Questions of the Bible:
Who? What? Where? When? Why?

Richard Edwin Craig, III

PUBLISH AMERICA

PublishAmerica
Baltimore

First printing

At the specific preference of the author, PublishAmerica allowed this work to remain exactly as the author intended, verbatim, without editorial input.

ISBN: 1-4241-1445-4
PUBLISHED BY PUBLISHAMERICA, LLLP
www.publishamerica.com
Baltimore

Printed in the United States of America

Dedication

This work is dedicated to our grandchildren: Christopher Jayden Perez, Nathanael Scott Craig, and Rebekah Olivia Craig, and to all other young children who ask who or what or where or when or why.

Given the inquisitiveness of children, we know that children will get their answers either vicariously or experientially. In so many cases, we pray they learn from the former.

Contents

Introduction

It is amazing that the mark of a person's intelligence can be measured by the questions he or she asks. It is not really necessary to have all the answers. Take a look in the boardrooms of some of the major corporations. There you'll find the leader of the group posing more questions than he or she provides answers. Questions are often broached to cause others to think about their processes; to think about the direction they are pursuing; to think about the course of action currently underway. The leaders, the great heads of corporations and states can lead through the inquiry process.

Questions are supposed to be inquiries about matters for which the inquirer does not have the answer. That is a general idea of questions, however, because there is always the rhetorical question where the answer is not only intuitive but known. In general, Questions, according to my *Webster's New World Dictionary*, are supposed to express a sense of doubt or uncertainty. I like that definition because it makes me hearken back to Watergate days. Do you remember that now famous way of posing a question that reminds the writer of John Dean and others? "What did he know, and when did he know it?" That became a household question. It echoes sometimes even in these days.

Shakespeare has us thinking "To be or not to be; that is the question."

Questions are what the inquisitive little ones continually bombard us with on a daily basis.

Sometimes questions are asked and we know when they are posed that there are no answers; certainly no answers are readily apparent.

In the education process, teachers and instructors ask questions to determine if the subject matter has been mastered. That's the essence of testing or evaluation. What is the square root of 144? What impact did the League of Nation have on early 20th Century world politics? What is the molecular structure of water?

In the Genesis account from the Bible, we find the very first question uttered or asked in human history. And there has been no end to the number and kinds of questions that have been posed since those early days in humankind's existence. Everything from "Do you love me?" to "What's for dinner?"

Each year at Lent, I think about some discipline, about some exercise I should pursue to enhance my knowledge, my understanding of the relationship that God has fostered with humankind and with me specifically. This series of meditations looks at some of the questions in Holy Scripture to see what they mean in the context they were written and what they mean to me and other people in this day and age.

The Bible is pregnant with all sorts of questions from the "Am I my brother's keeper?" to the hauntingly poignant, "Who do you say that I am?" God asked questions for which he already knew the answers. For example, God asked Cain the first child, "Where is your brother?" And despite the fact God knew the answer, he asked the question anyway. The stranger asked the women at the tomb, "Why do you seek the living among the dead?" And perhaps the most potent and powerful of all questions found in the Bible was asked by Pontius Pilate. He asked Jesus, "And what is truth?" How many treatises and exposés have been written about that question?

As a foundation and context in which to explore the questions in the Bible, I wrote brief meditations and delivered them during Noonday Prayers offered at Saint Luke's Episcopal Church during the Weekdays of Lent in 2004. That means that I limited myself to approximately 30 examinations of questions. I did not attempt to prioritize these, choosing instead to randomly treat various questions asked in biblical history. I have simply chosen the questions that intrigued me. Any number of others, any other selection process could be chosen by others doing this same project.

I ask you the reader to journey with me as you read my treatment of the questions of the Bible. Think about the ones I have chosen to determine if the questions have any impact on your lives, on your relationships, on your personal situation. Don't hesitate to answer the questions for yourself? Don't be afraid that you do not have the answers. There are still mysteries in the world. There is still the unknown. Questions are stimulating. We are expected to provide an answer based on our life's experience and our education. Some answers to questions are apparent, some answers are made only after exhaustive investigation and study, and sometimes answers are not forthcoming at all. But in spite of this, questions continue to be posed. In time and space, most questions receive some sort of answer. The questions found in the Bible share in this way, and I will explore some of the more prominent questions herein.

Richard Edwin Craig, III

Meditation on a Question found in Genesis 2:25-3:5

"Now the serpent was more crafty than any other wild animal that the LORD God had made. He said to the woman, 'Did God say, 'You shall not eat from any tree in the garden?'" (New Revised Standard Version) The Good News Version records it this way: "Now the snake was the most cunning animal that the Lord God had made. The snake asked the woman, 'Did God really tell you not to eat fruit from any tree in the garden?'"

This is the first question recorded in the Bible. The woman should have been wary of the questioner based simply on the type question asked. Of course God told those first inhabitants what they could eat and what they could not eat. Of course God set out the rules of life for those primitive people. So why the question?

But the serpent is by the description a most crafty animal. On the one hand he asked a rhetorical question. On the other hand, he asked a question that might have caused a person to begin to doubt. So many times I have heard people say something to this effect: "Perhaps I didn't hear it clearly, or correctly." Or they may suggest that they misinterpreted what was said or what they heard, what rules were enumerated, and the like.

In this Lenten season, we remember how Satan tempted Jesus in the desert. In the Lukan account of the temptation, the devil says to a famished Jesus, "If you are the Son of God, command this stone to become a loaf of bread." In another instance he said, "If you are the Son of God, throw yourself down from here, for it is written, 'He will command his angels concerning you, to protect you'..." Notice the preamble to what the devil tells Jesus to do. He says, "If you are the Son of God..." Just think of what changes in the course of history might have been wrought if Jesus had pondered for any length of time whether he was the Son of God. Just think what might have transpired if Jesus had acted on the preamble to the question. We may have witnessed the following: "Yes, I am the Son of God. Just you watch me in action." Fortunately for the world, Jesus got the question and the response right. Fortunately for the world he did not get sidetracked, which I suggest the devil attempted to do to him.

My wife and I bought our very first house when we were each 23 years old. We had only been married a couple of years. Ours was a small house, but we kept it immaculate and the pride of ownership showed in its maintenance. One day a cousin of mine came over to see us. We may have been having a party; I can't remember now. However, my cousin cornered me, led me to the bathroom where he closed the door, and he asked me this question: "You smoke, don't you?" Of course, at that time, I smoked like a chimney. But that was a question that should have raised some questions of my own—it did not. I was too naïve, and I played right into his hands. He then followed up

QUESTIONS FROM THE BIBLE

with an offer that I smoke some marijuana with him. I should have known something was not right. I was fully grown; I owned my own home, and I did not need to smoke in the bathroom like some high school kid. So why, I should have pondered, were we cloistered in the bathroom? His question about my smoking should have raised the proverbial red flag.

And so it is with the questioning of Satan. Such questions arise almost daily in some of our lives. Little boys planning or scheming to do something they should not do oftentimes will ask a playmate, "Are your parents at home?" Those of us who have gone through high school recall those 'slackers' who approached you and asked, "Did you do your homework last night?" You can almost hear the next question coming at you like a freight train. "I did not sleep well last night; can I copy your paper?" Or perhaps it is some other lame excuse with the same request. In the big cities of this country, in certain areas, it is not at all uncommon to be asked by a woman on a dark street, "Do you want to have a good time?" In the big city I have heard other questions like "Do you need a good watch or a microwave or a television?" That usually emanates from a peddler on the streets or from a person standing by his open car trunk in a shopping center parking lot.

Sometimes the question is even subtler. In the guise of customer service, the clerk asks, "Did you find everything you need?" How many times has such a question led us to go back for one or more additional items? Or to ask for something we did not see?

The deception in so many of these cases lies in the fact that the person already knows the answer to the question. He or she already knows the truth of what he is asking. The wise old serpent knew what God had commanded those early people in the Garden. The devil knew that Jesus is the Son of God. My cousin knew that I smoked cigarettes. But those questions they asked can be just little hooks to lead us to their destination.

Questions, according to my *Webster's New World Dictionary*, are supposed to express a sense of doubt or uncertainty. Nothing in any of the examples we have reviewed adheres to this aspect of questions. The questioners all knew the answers before they posed the questions. Leads us to surmise that something more is in store; something more is on the agenda.

Perhaps, if I am to present an even-handed look at such questions, one has to accept that sometimes these questions, though they lead to something else, are not sinister. Remember how Jesus quizzed Peter three times, asking Peter each time, "Peter, do you love me?" Of course, Peter answered affirmatively each time, but he became a little perturbed because of this repetition. The bottomline was that Jesus wanted Peter to feed His sheep or people. It was a charge that Jesus wanted to lay on Peter. And he wanted that charge to really register with Peter. He also wanted Peter to follow him; that was his final charge.

And still the fact remains that we probably should be aware that when such questions as the ones we've viewed—and many others—have been posed, some ulterior aim or goal in the background is more than likely apparent or should be. Does the term 'waiting for the other shoe to drop' resonate with you?

Meditation on a Question found in Genesis 4:8-16

"Then the LORD said to Cain, 'Where is your brother Abel?' He said, 'I do not know; am I my brother's keeper?'"

How many times have you heard people parrot Cain? All my life I have heard the non-initiated ask that same question; "Am I my brother's keeper?" I think it is interesting, first of all, to note that God never really responded to the question. Why? In part, that may be because God refused to 'dignify the question' as we often say. Another reflection on God's lack of response in all probability lies in the fact that the answer is self-evident or should be.

In the beginning when God created the world and humankind, God said that it was not right that the man whom he created first should be alone. If we were not to be our brother's keeper, wouldn't God's assertion have been folly? Consider the account about this from Genesis:

Then the LORD God said, 'It is not good that the man should be alone; I will make him a helper as his partner.' So out of the ground the LORD God formed every animal of the field and every bird of the air...but for the man there was not found a helper as his partner. So the LORD God caused a deep sleep to fall upon the man, and he slept; then he took one of his ribs and closed up its place with flesh. And the rib that the LORD God had taken from the man he made into a woman and brought her to the man. Then the man said, 'This at last is bone of my bones and flesh of my flesh; this one shall be called Woman, for out of Man this one was taken.' Therefore a man leaves his father and his mother and clings to his wife, and they become one flesh.

Humankind as a result was created for support of each other. A man and a woman relate in a certain way. Other relationships emanated from this primordial establishment of human relationships. So it is safe to conclude and it follows that we are indeed our brother's keeper.

John Donne dealt with this whole notion of man's dependence on one another. In his *Meditation XVII* he wrote the following excerpted words:

"All mankind is of one author, and is one volume; when one man dies, one chapter is not torn out of the book, but translated into a better language; and every chapter must be so translated...As therefore the bell that rings to a sermon, calls not upon the preacher only, but upon the congregation to come: so this bell calls us all: but how much more me, who am brought so near the door by this sickness...No man is an island, entire of it; every man is a piece of the continent, a part of the main. If a clod be washed away by the sea, Europe is the less, as well as if a promontory were, as well as if a manor of thy friend's or of thine own were...any man's death diminishes me, because I am involved in mankind; and therefore never send to know for whom the bell tolls; it tolls for thee."

When I was a kid, I recall singing the song,
"No man is an island; no man stands alone.
Each man's joy is joy to me. Each man's grief is my own.
We need one another. So I will defend;
each man as my brother; each man as my friend."
We were constantly reminded in this and other ways about our dependency upon one another.

What about those of us who are people of the Way, or Christians as we are now known? The Apostle Paul had some interesting viewpoints in this area. His point is clearly articulated in *The First Letter of Paul to the Corinthians*, chapter 12, where we find these points:

Now there are varieties of gifts, but the same Spirit; and there are varieties of services, but the same Lord; and there are varieties of activities, but it is the same God who activates all of them in everyone. To each is given the manifestation of the Spirit for the common good...For just as the body is one and has many members, and all the members of the body, though many, are one body, so it is with Christ. For in the one Spirit we were all baptized into one body—Jews or Greeks, slaves or free—and we were all made to drink of one Spirit. Indeed, the body does not consist of one member but of many. If the foot would say, 'Because I am not a hand, I do not belong to the body,' that would not make it any less a part of the body. And if the ear would say, 'Because I am not an eye, I do not belong to the body,' that would not make it any less a part of the body. If the whole body were an eye, where would the hearing be? If the whole body were hearing, where would the sense of smell be? But as it is, God arranged the members in the body, each one of them, as he chose. If all were a single member, where would the body be? As it is, there are many members, yet one body. The eye cannot say to the hand, 'I have no need of you,' nor again the head to the feet, 'I have no need of you.' On the contrary, the members of the body that seem to be weaker are indispensable, and those members of the body that we think less honorable we clothe with greater honor, and our less respectable members are treated with greater respect; whereas our more respectable members do not need this. But God has so arranged the body, giving the greater honor to the inferior member, that there may be no dissension within the body, but the members may have the same care for one another. If one member suffers, all suffer together with it; if one member is honored, all rejoice together with it.

If you recall an episode in *The Gospel According to Mark*, the brothers Zebedee, James and John, told Jesus they wanted him to grant them the right to sit one at his right and the other at his left in his Glory. Jesus took that opportunity to teach them and the other disciples that those who would be great would be slaves or servants of all. There is that interdependence again. The Servant Song is a wonderful song for representing this point of view and this truth about how and why we exist with and among each other. It also is often used during the footwashing services on Maundy Thursday to underscore and highlight the whole matter or servanthood. Verse 2 is so appropriate to our topic of discussion and says

We are pilgrims on a journey.
We are brothers on the road.

We are here to help each other
Walk the mile and bear the load.

Throughout the centuries of humankind's existence, we have formulated all sorts of creedal statements about our relationships to one another. The League of Nations, the United Nations, and other political organizations are attempts, it seems, to flesh out the truth that we are our brother's keeper. I love the creed, "Together we stand; divided we fall. One for all, and all for one!" Do you like "We're all in this together?"

Our Lord Jesus made it perfectly clear what our relationship to others should be. He gave us a new commandment. In *The Gospel According to John* we find this commandment: "I give you a new commandment, that you love one another. Just as I have loved you, you also should love one another." (13:34) Clearly we must exercise some concern for our fellow man and woman. It is not sufficient that we concentrate on ourselves solely. Even the Lone Ranger had his faithful companion.

Obviously Cain did not have the benefit of the hindsight and all the experience to reflect on human relationships that we have in this day. Had such been available to him, he might not have posed the question. But then again, humans often attempt to sidetrack an issue; to remove the spotlight that is on us; to obfuscate the truth.

God did not answer Cain's question, but we have answered it this day. There is no doubt among rational men and women today that we, like Cain, are our brother's keeper. The prayer of many is or becomes that given this understanding of our connectedness, we will learn to live out that truth in the world among the various peoples of the world, among the peoples within our own countries, among the peoples of our state, among those in our cities and communities, and in our families. Am I my brother's keeper? You bet I am, and so too are you.

Meditation on a Question found in John 8:1-11

"Teacher, this woman has been caught in the act of adultery. Now the Law of Moses commanded us to stone such. What do you say about her?" (RSV)

There are so many questions that arise in my mind as I sort through this episode. First, how did these men happen to come upon this woman "in the act of adultery?" (Or in the words of the *Good News* translation, "In the very act of committing adultery") Had she been suspected of such activity previously, and her discovery was the result of a stakeout? Did someone happen to arrive at home unexpectedly? My son who looks at some of the modern day descendants of those Middle Eastern peoples would ask, "Why weren't those men at work?" No doubt you have questions of your own. Most women looking at this story are puzzled as to why the man she was with was not also brought to Jesus. This latter question can probably be dismissed based on the fact that adultery was not necessarily the same for men and women. We'll just leave it at that for our purposes.

What is apparent is that a group of men were zealously and adamantly determined to see that this woman paid the price for her adultery. I guess the most important question about this event is why did they bring her to Jesus? They already knew what the Law of Moses mandated in such instances. Scripture tells us that the scribes and the Pharisees were setting forth a test, and they sought something for which they could charge Jesus. So it appears they were not seeking righteousness at all. They were seeking to remove Jesus as an influential figure. With Jesus out of the picture, these Jewish officials, no doubt, might regain the status that they obviously had lost as a result of Jesus having entered their space.

I have always loved the way Jesus responds to his enemies. I love the way he answers a question with a question. I love the way he answers a question by not answering it at all. In this particular case, Jesus did not address the question at all. He did not, however, say anything contrary to what is found in the Law of Moses. After prodding, and as the men became more insistent, Jesus relented and spoke his mind about the situation. He did not say that the punishment was too severe for the sin committed. He did not say that there should be no punishment. What he did say was this: "Let him who is without sin among you be the first to throw a stone at her."

There you have it. The stoning can begin. Jesus has spoken. He simply added a little caveat that the initial stoning commence at the hands of the one among the group who is without sin. Now as we read the old scripture, we find that it is written that "All we like sheep have gone astray." The psalmist said, "If you, Lord, were to note what is done amiss, O Lord, who could stand?" (Psalm 130:2)

Jesus did not say it, but if I had been there I might have uttered, "Gotcha!"

Not a single person could honestly have tossed the stone to begin the execution. They, like all of us, were flawed. Certainly they had missed the mark on more than one occasion. They had been separated from God by what they had done and by what they had left undone. They had sinned in thought, word, and deed.

Jesus taught a valuable lesson that day. He spoke about judgment, and punishment, and grace, and how God looks at us. I am most often reminded of the Canticle we use in the Daily Office, the Second Song of Isaiah. It says

Let the wicked forsake their ways *
and the evil ones their thoughts;
And let them turn to the Lord, and he will have compassion, *
and to our God, for he will richly pardon.
For my thoughts are not your thoughts, *
nor your ways my ways, says the Lord.
For as the heavens are higher than the earth, *
so are my ways higher than your ways,
and my thoughts than your thoughts.

When all the persons who had brought the woman to Jesus had left, he asked her, "Where are your accusers?" He asked her if any had condemned her. Then he told her that neither did he accuse her. He told her to go and sin no more.

I also think about John 3:16-17, that most powerful passage from one of the great gospels. I'll never forget an episode of the television program, Lou Grant, which was on the air a number of years ago. Seems that some members of that mythical newsroom had been the victims of a scam by a man they all had respected. I recall the publisher, I believe he was, saying about the con man, "I want to get my pound of flesh." Seems to me that's where the scribes and Pharisees were relative to the woman. But in that powerful passage from John, we read these words: "For God so loved the world that he gave his only Son, that whoever believes in him should not perish but have eternal life. For God sent the Son into the world, not to condemn the world, but that the world might be saved through him."

That's a different approach to judgment. Those men who brought the woman before Jesus were not aware of this new way of looking at the human condition. Jesus taught an important lesson to those of us who have ears to hear. Perhaps those men did not recognize what Jesus did that day, but certainly those of us who are Christians have seen the justice of his approach. Our ways are not God's ways. That's what we would say to the scribes and Pharisees. We should also say that God's mercy and compassion and forgiveness can and, thankfully, does transcend the Law.

Jesus' actions on that fateful day underscore what has also been written. That is, that God does not desire the death of any sinner. He wants us to repent and return to him. The men asked Jesus, "What do you say about her?" Jesus said volumes in his actions on that day.

Meditation on a Question found in John 20:1-18

"They said to her, 'Woman, why are you weeping?'"

Jesus also asked the same question of her to which Mary Magdalene had a perfectly good answer. She replied that they (I wonder who 'they' are) had taken away her Lord, and she did not know where he had been laid. The word perplexity comes to mind. So too does the word dismay. Aloneness is a third word. And confusion. At least Mary had a reason for weeping.

God did some wonderful things with the human body, and with the human soul. Crying is one of those wonderful things built into the personage of everyone. Ever hear the phrase, 'a good cry?' What is a good cry? You know; it's the kind that upon completion, a person feels much, much better. That's a good cry.

And people cry for various reasons. Given the text we are considering, it would be easy to think of crying simply in the context of a death or other loss. And that is an important time for crying. Mary was at a loss. The master had been killed, and now he was even MIA, so to speak. 'Where have they laid him,'

RICHARD EDWIN CRAIG, III

she pondered. No longer having that person in her life was almost more than she could handle. I, being an orphan now, can resonate with Mary and all the other people who weep following the loss of a loved one. The heart, when it is hurting, just elicits a good cry. It is almost inevitable.

A little child shall lead them. It is to such as these that the Kingdom of Heaven belongs. Unless you come as a little child... You get the idea. And I got an idea about this matter of what caused Mary to cry. Sure, she was sad. We are all sad when someone we love and adore and care for dies. This feeling can even be seen in the animal world. Ever see a photo of a little dog standing guard over a fallen playmate?

Mary cried because Jesus had to die in God's scheme of salvation for us. Some of those tears may have been shed because Mary was concerned about the rightness of that approach. Here's what a little boy said about a particular sacrifice that may bear on our situation. In *Children's Letters to God*, the boy wrote:

Dear God,
If you let The dinasor
not exstinct we would
not have a country.
You did the right thing.
Jonathan

Jonathan reasoned correctly that if the dinosaurs had not become extinct, then humankind might not have been able to coexist or indeed long endure. Perhaps the two species would have been adversaries and man may have lost out. In any event,

Jonathan observes that a purpose was attached to the extinction of those ancient creatures. In that same way, Jesus had to die for our sins. It was the way that God planned to author our salvation. In time, no doubt, Mary came to that realization and her tears were wiped away. In fact, it was not long at all after her discovery that she encountered the risen Lord.

Why are you weeping? That is the question posed to Mary. In our lives we have been asked the same question or something akin to it. There is something interesting about crying. We do it for a number of reasons and not just at times of sadness. Tears of joy are shed more times than we can count. Look at the Academy Awards just recently aired on television. Many of the recipients shed a few tears on that glittering evening. Tears are shed when we are physically hurt. How many mothers have kissed the banged up finger of a little child who weeps until he is sufficiently soothed?

But crying elicits some strange reactions as well. Perhaps what I share next with you is a cultural thing, but as I travel across the country, I find similar episodes among the people of this nation. I have heard a mother say to a crying child, "You'd better stop that crying or I'll give you something to cry about?" Is that the proverbial double bind that Psychologists talk about? How many fathers have told their little boys, "Men don't cry?" That mantra may have created more monsters than we care to think about.

But to weep is a natural occurrence. It is not relegated to any one sex, culture, or the like. I will never forget as a young boy that I cried at a scene in a movie on the Armchair Playhouse of the 1950's. In the movie, a soldier in a foxhole was killed. His buddy stood over his fallen comrade and sang the song, 'My Buddy." I just boohooed! How many veterans of our various wars can avoid a tear at various events of remembrance for those who died for us? Despite how some artists have depicted our Lord, he had to be a 'tough cookie' to have withstood the rigors of traveling all over his world—on foot! Yet at the grave of his friend, Jesus wept.

The angels asked Mary why she was weeping, and that was altogether appropriate. We cry for different reasons. In her case, however, her weeping was not necessary because the permanent death that she feared and the misplacement of the body were not reality. Jesus had been raised from the dead; he was no longer in any grave. That said, why are you weeping is a good question.

Weeping can be done in monumental proportion. Do you recall the song "Cry me a River?" Our whole nation cried collectively on the occasion of Nine One One. No shame was attached to tears at that time. No creedal statements were evoked in deference to those who wept.

Those of us who are weeping now, why is that? Does it have anything to do with a war in Iraq or Afghanistan or in the Middle East? Is our jobs situation unsolvable? Do we rely too heavily on secular solutions as opposed to sacred ones? Are poverty and hunger and disease still among us despite our advances in the sciences? Can we take a moment or two to reflect on our grief? Is our situation untenable? Is it without hope? Is the Lord working for us? Don't we comprehend that all things work together for good for those who love the Lord? Are these and other situations causes for our weeping?

Like Mary, if we get certain truth, we may find that there is no need to shed any tears. We may find also that God has worked in our lives to wipe away our tears. Why do we continue to weep? Perhaps we need to recite—and understand—a portion of that great psalm once more:

I lift up my eyes to the hills—from where will my help come?
My help comes from the Lord, who made heaven and earth.
Psalm 121:1

In the face of such reality, it may become less and less necessary for people to ask us why we are weeping. It may become less and less necessary for us to weep. The angels asked Mary, "Woman, why are you weeping?"

Meditation on a Question found in John 5:1-9b

"One man was there who had been ill for thirty-eight years. When Jesus saw him lying there and knew that he had been there a long time, he said to him, 'Do you want to be made well?'"

At first glance, what a ridiculous question Jesus asked of the man at the pool. Who, in his right mind, would not want to be made well? Who, in his right mind, would want to continue to be in pain, or to be disabled, or unable to function normally, or to be a person of unclean lips and body? Who? So, on the surface, one has to wonder about the question that Jesus raised in this story.

But don't count Jesus out just yet. Remember that he is like E. F. Hutton, in some respects. When he speaks, people listen, even his enemies. What he says is usually pregnant with meaning. Do you want to be made well? I simply assumed-there it is-that any person afflicted with an illness would want to be cured. Anecdotally, I would wish that for myself. Not too many years ago, I became very ill. Since my recovery, my wife and daughter have commented on that illness. They were fearful of my condition and were anxious for my recovery.

I recall during that illness that I used to go to a separate place where I wrote poetry in menu form under water. It was a place I consciously entered at will. At least I thought I entered that place. It was all so real to me. In retrospect, I understand that the fever I had probably contributed to that state of consciousness or unconsciousness.

I have a couple of addictions. One of those is overeating. I can recall making comments about persons suffering from the kinds of illnesses that leave them without an appetite. I asserted that I could never be in a state of not being able to eat. Well, this illness proved me wrong. During that illness, I lost interest in food. Food no longer tasted good to me, and I stopped eating. Marie was really worried. Then I began to consider the merits of not eating, i.e., losing weight and all the attending benefits of that process (when done properly). I did not want to change my position on eating, and the result was that I ate very little and lost some weight.

Now the question becomes clearer to me, or rather the purpose becomes clearer. Do you want to be made well? In some ways, I really did want to be made well; in others, I was quite apathetic about the whole affair.

Sick people in many instances receive a good deal of sympathy and attention. I even recall a time in my childhood when that fact was brought home to me very dramatically. A friend of my sister broke his leg. I recall that all the girls signed his cast. They paid a lot of attention to him. I recall, even at my tender age, recognizing that attention and wanting the same for myself.

Do you want to be made well? It is a good question after all, I believe. When a person's condition changes, then that person may be expected to return to normalcy, whatever that may have been for him or her. That person will be expected to return to his duties, his job, to function as he did prior to the onset of the illness. That person may now have to do for himself: cook his own food, make his bed, and the like. Excuses that once prefaced any comments about that person are discontinued. Being well means that person has to return to the mainstream of life. One who is made well will now have to be a player in life. And, persons who don't want to return to the expectancies of life may not relish the thought of being made well. Jesus knows that, and so he asks that question. The man in the account in Luke had been ill for years, 38 to be exact. What had he been doing in all those years? Who had waited on him? Who cared for him? If he was now made well, what would he be expected to do? Jesus no doubt had some insight into this man's life and his state of mind. So, Jesus questioned the man.

A typical human type answer was given by the man to Jesus. He made it everyone else's fault that he could not get into the pool. Jesus let him off the hook on that score, but Jesus healed the man, and we know that his life was never the same again. That is true on two levels. First, the man could live out the rest of his life like all other healthy individuals. Second, being touched by Jesus in any way, but especially through healing, generates a great need and urgency to make the appropriate response or responses. When Jesus touches our lives, we are not the same. Healing is just one of the ways that Jesus prepares us to continue in his earthly ministry, the restoration of all people to unity with God and each other in Christ.

So, when you approach God on this day or any other day, will it be to be made well? Or, will you have another unspoken agenda? If you go in answer to Jesus' question, which he asks of us, then know that an affirmative answer means that you are willing, able and prepared to get back into the game of life as a witness of Christ Jesus.

It would be good for such persons to consider how long they have been ill. Consider how long they have been afflicted. Consider how their condition in life has left them on the sidelines. Consider how much they really want to love and serve the Lord. Then say, "Yes, yes Jesus! I want to be made well." Come quickly Lord Jesus and when we have been made whole again; enlist us to your service.

When we say yes, understand that we will no longer be the same; we will be strong and fit as for battle. We will know the truth of what we sometimes say as we close out the Eucharist: that the service for all able-bodied persons now begins, thanks be to God. AMEN.

Meditation on a Question found in Matthew 27:45-56

"Eli, Eli, lema sabachthani?" that is, "My God, my God, why have you forsaken me?"

The campsite for the Girl Scouts was located in an isolated—I'd even say desolate—location far away from the paved, well-traveled national highway. But getting to that location for this mother and daughter was no problem as they drove in caravan with other mothers and chauffeurs of girls who were also attending that overnight event.

When this particular mother unloaded her daughter, said her good-byes, and cranked up her car for the return trip home, she quickly discerned that the others who had come down with her had departed without her. Now it was incumbent upon this mother to make her journey back to Highway 90 all by herself. Perhaps in this modern age that might not be such a big deal; however, in that area several miles from that major highway, there were no lights on that dirt road and no hints even of civilization. There were lots of scary things lurking in the dark, like animals and men who wore sheets over their heads, and there were no communications or call boxes along the way if that mother had broken down or found herself in need of assistance for other reasons.

Generally, the moon shines brightly in that part of the country, and it normally would illumine the countryside as well as the sky. But such was not the case that particular evening. It was pitch black dark. How else could one describe it?

The ordeal of getting back to the highway was an experience that this mother thought at first she would have to endure alone. The prospects of that must have been horrifying! In all likelihood, she must have cried out to those who had been her companions. In all likelihood, she must have cried out at them as well. Why had they left her in harm's way? Why had they not continued to travel with her along this perilous path? Why had she been left to her own designs, to her own imagination, and to her own strength, to endure what would transpire till she reached the journey's end? These and perhaps many, many other thoughts and questions no doubt were raised in her mind. In the silences of her soul, she felt betrayed. She felt abandoned. She felt that a guarantee had not been upheld. So journey on she did.

When Jesus went to Bethany because his friend Lazarus had died, Jesus prayed to God the Father in this manner. "Jesus looked upwards and said, 'Father, I thank you for having heard me. I knew that you always hear me, but I have said this for the sake of the crowd standing here, so that they may believe that you sent me.' When he had said this, he cried with a loud voice, 'Lazarus, come out!' The dead man came out, his hands and feet bound with strips of cloth, and his face wrapped in a cloth. Jesus said to them, 'Unbind him, and let him go.'" That was what Jesus had come to expect. He relied upon the Father, and his father answered his prayers. His Father worked in harmony and unison with him. His father did not abandon him or leave him alone in that situation.

Jesus often found himself surrounded by a great cloud of onlookers, seekers, disciples, and the hungry both spiritually as well as physically. It was on a given day that his great preaching and teaching had caused a huge crowd to gather. When Jesus had finished his lecture/sermon, it was too late for the people to go to the neighboring towns and villages to get food. But among those present was a lad who had brought a sack lunch from home. But what was so little to so many? In what must have been a strange request, the people followed instructions and sat in specific configurations and groups in the green grass. "Taking the five loaves and the two fish, he looked up to heaven, and blessed and broke the loaves, and gave them to his disciples to set before the people; and he divided the two fish among them all. And all ate and were filled; and they took up twelve baskets full of broken pieces and of the fish. Those who had eaten the loaves numbered five thousand men." (Mark 6:41-44) This was another example of God the Father's faithfulness to his son in his earthly ministry.

In our modern age, we have become accustomed to performance guarantees. Especially in the area of products, we have certain expectations. In fact, such performance is mandated as well as expected in the products of certain manufacturers. So assured are some manufacturers in the ability of their products to provide continuous and flawless service and performance that warrantees and guarantees have reached previously unheard of levels. With automobiles, for examples, the ten-year warranty is becoming a standard. The old adage—that cars are maintenance free till the final payment has been made—is now a relic of the past.

Before those three hours on that Friday afternoon, Jesus had walked a path littered with those who shouted all kinds of epithets at him. Only a couple of people had the decency along the way to provide him any comfort and assistance. There was Veronica who wiped his face and Simon Cyrene who carried the cross a ways. But few others were sympathetic to this man's plight. Most surely, many along the path to the cross knew who this man was. Surely many of them recalled how the crowds cheered him as he rode into Jerusalem. Many of them also had screamed for his execution. "Crucify him!" they had shouted over and over again. One can't help but think about the hymn, "Alone thou goest forth O Lord, in sacrifice to die." Since that time another hymn has been written that asks, "Must Jesus bear the cross alone and all the world go free? No, there's a cross for everyone, and there's a cross for me." But on that dark day, Jesus would have to go it alone.

If we performed a flashback, we'd find that Jesus had looked to his father for a certain performance. He expected that his Father would accompany him in the perilous waters of this earthly mission and ministry. Almost as if considering his life to be propagated by the Father, Jesus now found that life span to be in jeopardy. The human Jesus hang on the hardwood of the cross. Men had not been able to discern who he was. It's ironic that the Negro spiritual "Sweet little Jesus Boy" tells us they did not know who he was at Bethlehem, and now we see they did not know who he was at Calvary. Men had refused to accept who he was because he threatened their authority and the status quo. But regardless of what men thought or did not think, Jesus looked to God the Father for his longevity, for his safety. Where was that heavenly performance guarantee? Jesus hang there on that cross, and when he looked down, only a handful of people who knew him, who were his friends or relatives, dared stand in the shadow of that wooden implement of shame and death. On that old rugged cross, he knew that he was like the athlete who plays tennis. From the opening serve in Pilate's palace, Jesus discovered that he would not receive coaching; he would not receive any help from his mentor. The game was now his to play in solo. He'd have to muster up all the faithfulness he had acquired in his earthly ministry. The performance guarantee was now his to execute and make good. It was in that context, no doubt, that Jesus uttered this cry, "Eli, Eli, lema sabachthani?" that is, "My God, my God, why have you forsaken me?"

Meditation on a Question found in Psalm 121

"I lift up my eyes to the hills—from where will my help come?"

This is one of our grand psalms. It is positive in every way. There is none of that stuff about me or someone else going down to the pit. There is none of that stuff about vanquishing my enemies. There is none of that stuff about a betrayal at the hands of a good friend. What we have in this psalm is an affirmation about where we can look when we sing songs of bleakness, of despair, and of puzzlement. Immediately coming to my memory is a song that was very popular a number of years ago. It went something like this. "Who can I turn to when nobody needs me? My heart wants to know and so I must go where destiny leads me. With no star to guide me, and no one beside me. I'll go on my way, and after the day, the darkness will hide me…" That's a pretty sad song. Sad in that the composer is not aware of the help that exists for him, indeed for all of us.

In frivolous matters, in matters of the mundane, help is usually just a fingertip away. We can look into our yellow pages for someone to come and "fix it" if we have a problem. The condition of the hardwood floors in the house we recently purchased was atrocious. A lack of maintenance was obvious, and the kids were apparently permitted to be as creative as they wished with things like paint. We contacted several companies who specialized in refinishing hardwood floors. We settled on one, and the work done has added a tremendous value to our home. For those kinds of needs, it is not incumbent upon us to ring our hands and agonize over our problems.

But when we do not have the money to have our air conditioner repaired, or when we do not have sufficient money to buy groceries for the family, or when someone in the family needs an operation and we have no insurance; those are the kinds of difficulties that cause us to ask the question, "From where will my help come?" When we feel spiritually bankrupt, to whom do we turn? When our marriage is on the rocks, who offers the best solutions? Those critical needs in our life that seem on the surface to have no solution require 'strong medicine.'

Jane is not one of those persons who are ignorant about matters of help. She is a little girl who wrote a letter to God. In one of my favorites, *Children's Letters to God*, Jane writes this question: "In Sunday School they told us what you do. Who does it when you are on vacation?" Her inquiry gives us an understanding that there may be a need for continuance, and she would just like to know what arrangements God makes for handling things while he is away. But she probably knows that God helps us in times of need.

Psalm 121 asks that question about where one's help emanates, and then provides an answer. Surprise, surprise! "My help comes from the LORD, who made heaven and earth. He will not let your foot be moved; he who keeps you will not slumber. He who keeps Israel will neither slumber nor sleep. The LORD is your keeper; the LORD is your shade at your right hand. The sun shall not strike you by day, nor the moon by night. The LORD will keep you from all evil; he will keep your life. The LORD will keep your going out and your coming in from this time on and forevermore."

Jane knows about the kind of help that is available to us. The psalmist understood it as well. But isn't it interesting that sometimes we do not consider that reality in our lives? We sometimes pursue solutions in our own strength.

Many years ago, I got into a financial crunch. I, being the intelligent person who has been raised in the ethos of the culture of the United States of America, looked to myself, to my own devices and designs to free me from the bounds in which I found myself. I learned quickly that no matter how often creditors indicate that they want to work with people, that is not necessarily so. It is especially not the case for certain creditors. It was not until I turned over my financial situation to God that resolution was forthcoming. I asked the right question: "Where is my help to come?" But I accepted the wrong answer initially. My help, your help, our help always comes from the Lord who made heaven and earth. That is true in simple things and in complex matters as well.

A friend of mine was a computer programmer. He told me about the time he was working on a most difficult programming problem. Nothing he tried worked. In desperation he turned to God [A good choice, I suggest]. He uttered a prayer, asking God to send him the solution to his problem. In an instant the answer came to him, but my friend did not realize from whom the answer came. When the answer presented itself, my friend said, "Never mind God, I just thought of the answer."

On the way to the office this morning, I saw a young woman with a little girl. They were obviously preparing to get into their minivan or SUV. When I first saw this duo, the little girl was throwing some debris into the street. The mother, probably acting instinctively pursued the objects in the middle of the street. Simultaneously, the little girl ran down the street. Frantically, the mother, having retrieved the thrown objects, pursued the little girl. As I moved toward the stop and go light, I looked in my rear view mirror to see the mother safely putting the little child into the vehicle. I thought: "What if she had more than one energetic child?" Many people do. Who watches over the caregivers of children? No cars were coming down the street. Thank God! I am reminded again of what the psalmist asserted. "The LORD will keep you from all evil; he will keep your life. The LORD will keep your going out and your coming in from this time on and forevermore."

The church is the Body of Christ in the world. Jesus came that we might have life and have it abundantly. Now that government is no longer in the helping business, addressing the needs of the poor, and the homeless, and the naked, and the incarcerated, has become one of the priorities of the church once again. Many people have come to the knowledge that the churches can answer their question about from where their help will come. Christ has no body but ours, and ours are the hands of Christ in the world. It is natural—and expected—that those associated with the Body of Christ will work to provide for others who are in any need.

A young man sought my counsel and ministering when he was in jail. The checkbook for my discretionary fund has many stubs representing help we have been able to give to individuals in Racine since my arrival in this town. The Sacrament of Healing, Unction, is offered weekly to those who are ill.

No matter how big or how small a problem may be, it is clear that God can be instrumental in bringing resolution. In this Lenten season, we even focus on the fact that there is help for those of us who have sinned against God and their neighbor. The so-called comfortable words pronounced during Rite One of the Eucharist provide clear, unequivocal answers to the question posed by the psalmist, to wit: "from where will my help come?" Hear those comfortable words again.

Come unto me, all ye that travail and are heavy laden, and I will refresh you. *Matthew 11:28*

God so loved the world, that he gave his only-begotten Son, to the end that all that believe in him should not perish, but have everlasting life. *John 3:16*

This is a true saying, and worthy of all men to be received, that Christ Jesus came into the world to save sinners. *1 Timothy 1:15*

If any man sin, we have an Advocate with the Father, Jesus Christ the righteous; and he is the perfect offering for our sins, and not for ours only, but for the sins of the whole world. *1 John 2:1-2*

I thank God that for many of us we know instinctively and through experience the answer to the psalmist's question. "I lift up my eyes to the hills—from where will my help come?" Now it becomes our duty to share that knowledge with those who labor in ignorance to that truth.

Meditation on a Question found in Genesis 3:8-19

"Where are you? Who told you that you were naked? Have you eaten of the tree of which I commanded you not to eat?" Genesis 3:8-19

We speak of God as being omniscient. When we look up that term, we find a reference to God, to wit: "[Omniscient means] having universal knowledge; knowing all things; infinitely knowing or wise; as, the omniscient God." All-knowing, and yet, God asks questions of his newly created humans. Where are you? Who told you that you were naked? Have you eaten of the tree of which I commanded you not to eat? Why? Why did God inquire about matters of which he obviously was already aware and knew the answers?

One of our sons had a very primitive sense of what was and what was not revealed. I will not disclose which of the two boys had this problem. My wife made me aware of this however. It seems this son wanted to hide from her, so he ducked behind an object of furniture. Marie called him repeatedly, but he did not answer because he thought she did not know where he was. The irony in this situation is that only his head and shoulders were obscured from view. The rest of his body was in plain view. This little child laughed to himself because he obviously thought that since he could not see Marie that she could not see him.

Adam hid from God. He hid from the person who had made all the heavens and the earth, the animals, and finally his helpmate, Eve. And in spite of that revelation, Adam thought that he might be able to hide from God. Such a primitive assumption, and akin to our son who was a tot at the time.

The word that comes to my mind as I read these questions is rhetorical. "A rhetorical question is one asked solely to produce an effect (especially to make an assertion) rather than to elicit a reply."

What effect was God attempting to produce in Adam? We know that God already knew the answer, and it appears that this episode departs from the norm in that God sought a particular reply: the truth. There appears little doubt that God wanted a confession from Adam.

I guess I have watched too much television over the years. I have also spent many years as most of us have in public education settings. How many times in police movies, for example, have you heard a police official say to a suspect, "Tell the truth and it will go easier on you?" I recall teachers using similar admonitions with children who were possibly perpetrators of some sort of misdeed in or out of the classroom. "Did you hit Johnny?" "How did that Nintendo get into your locker?"

God knew well the character of the serpent—he made him. God was aware that the serpent had a silver tongue. He was smooth. He was charming, no doubt. He could be convincing. What Adam and Eve had done was probably not a surprise given the presence of the serpent in the garden.

But God wanted some honest answers. He probably would have preferred that Adam confess to what he had done without having been asked. Forgive me Father for I have sinned. God knows that we have sinned. He knows that we have missed the mark. He knows that we have not followed in the ways he has set out for us. Why don't we come clean? Why did Adam wait for God to bring up the subject of their hiding, their having eaten of fruit of which they were commanded not to eat, or their being naked? Why do we put off these matters? God already knows our transgressions and our sins.

"Nothing is covered up that will not be uncovered, and nothing secret that will not become known. Therefore whatever you have said in the dark will be heard in the light, and what you have whispered behind closed doors will be proclaimed from the housetops." Luke 12:2-3 In effect, Jesus is saying here that what is committed in the dark will come out in the light. We have only to search our own lives to recall things in our life that we concealed, but which eventually came to light. In a daytime soap opera, a group of men have kept a secret for 30 years. Seems a young girl in their car, when they were teenagers, drowned in a car accident. Rather than come clean, the men made a pact to keep the secret. However, this soap rightly portrays what happens to secrets. Sooner of later, the truth will be known.

Regarding secrets, there appears to be innately within us the need to dispel or to disclose those secrets we hang onto. Some secrets go to the grave with some people, but judgment probably demands confession in the hereafter. The Fram commercial said, "Pay me now or pay me later."

How long did Adam think he could hide from God? Did he think he could hide from God the truth of what he and his helpmate had done? Was he prepared to answer those questions which God finally broached? My wife was raised as an only child. She has told me on numerous times how as a little girl she wondered how her folks knew that she had done something. From a childish point of view, that's the downside of being an only child—there is no one on whom to shift the blame. There is one thing for sure about Adam's situation; he could not shift the blame too much, although he did try to make Eve the heavyweight in this episode.

So can anything good come out of reflecting on these questions today? That's like asking if anything good can come out of Nazareth. This is the season of Lent, and what better time do we have to reflect on how we have separated ourselves from God? Those same kinds of questions that God asked Adam can be asked of us in somewhat modified form. Where are we? In our loving God and loving our neighbor? Where are we? In our proclaiming of the good news of God in Christ through word and example. Where are we? In our serving Christ in all persons? Where are we? In our working for justice and peace? Where are we? In our feeding the hungry, clothing the naked, and housing the homeless? Where are we?

Have you eaten the forbidden fruit? Who among us can say no to that question? That question is about our not living our lives in the context of having been made in the image of God. Sin is what each of us has committed.

God already knows these things about us. Remember he is omniscient. He asks those questions of all humankind the fact that he knows the answers notwithstanding. He is eliciting the utterance of the truth. He really hopes that we will make a confession to him before he has a chance to ask us. In matters of sin and 'missing the mark,' remember the Ash Wednesday lesson from *Joel*. "Yet even now, says the LORD, return to me with all your heart, with fasting, with weeping, and with mourning; rend your hearts and not your clothing. Return to the LORD, your God, for he is gracious and merciful, slow to anger, and abounding in steadfast love, and relents from punishing. Who knows whether he will not turn and relent, and leave a blessing behind him, a grain offering and a drink offering for the LORD, your God?"

God, I am hiding from you. It is the human condition in the face of our sin. The serpent told me that I was naked. And yes, I have tasted the fruit which it was not right for me to eat. But I come to you seeking your mercy. Have mercy on me your creation. Do not let your anger burn toward me. I have turned again to you. Will you grant me absolution? That, it seems, is the kind of response that God sought from Adam and that he seeks from us today.

Meditation on a Question found in Mark 10:35-45

"What do you want me to do for you?"

O the possibilities! Here is a man who can grant one's every wish, and he has asked, "What do you want me to do for you?" An open-ended question. No strings attached. The field, seemingly, is wide open. What does one request?

I wonder if people are truly honest when they speak about wishes. When the odds of getting struck by lightning are greater than winning a state lottery, or when one's chance of winning a lottery is some astronomical odd—like 3 or 4 million to one, then that reality just might color what people say about what they'd do if they won a major lottery.

Once I heard a bishop of the church say that if he won the Powerball, which we have access to in Wisconsin, he'd spread the money among the churches so that priests could be placed without being concerned about monetary compensation. In other words, a priest would make a livable wage whether he served a big parish or a small mission. I think we can see the ramifications of that, and that would be a good thing.

How many times, when the jackpot of a particular lottery has grown extremely high, have you heard people speak about the altruistic things they would do if they won the big jackpot? "I'll give money to my church." "I'd give money to my favorite charity." One person I know said that in the spirit of an old television show, the Millionaire, he would give thousands of dollars to unsuspecting individuals—no strings attached.

I don't engage in such talk because I am like the man who prayed to God for the winning combination of numbers for the lottery. After a frustrating time of not winning the lottery, the man prayed to God and asked, "Why have you not granted me the winning numbers for the lottery?" To which God replied, "You could help me out if you bought a ticket."

Perhaps, it is the human condition in me, but I confess to you that I would think about my past and all the things I have had to do without; all the things my kids can use now; the exotic vacation I have never taken; a car that runs not only 24/7 but everyday in the year. I argue with my son, who is a part of the younger generation that feels the days of Social Security are numbered. It would be good to be in a position where Social Security's existence does not matter.

John and James and the blind man were all honest about what they wanted. That is not to say that those who purportedly would spend their winnings elsewhere are not telling the truth. It is all probably a matter of winning the lottery being an incomprehensible, unimaginable occurrence for the average person. If such persons actually won some big money, things just might be different.

Jesus said that he came that we might have life and have it abundantly. If he asks us what he can do for us, why would we not tell him what we really want?

Jesus also taught us in the prayer we now revere to ask for our daily bread, or the things we need to sustain our lives each day. That, it seems, would include necessities as well as some of the more frivolous or the mundane, even the pleasurable.

John and James asked Jesus to grant them the privilege of sitting by his side in his glory, one at his right and the other at his left. Who wouldn't want to be in that position? However, I now think about what it means to sit at the right hand as opposed to sitting at the left. Contemplate the concept of the right hand man. Do you not know the Christian tradition that Jesus having ascended to the Father stands at the right hand of God where he is interceding for us? But consider the position. John and James asked for those positions, but had their wishes been granted, how would they have settled who would have sat where?

Seems some things have a real chance of being effected, and others carry some consequence or may not be grantable. As a little boy, I remember that I understood that God would answer my prayers. I recall praying for a new book satchel, which I received [and by the way, which I slept with one night].

Jesus made it perfectly clear that some things he was not in a position to grant. Some things fall in the domain of the Father. And such were the positions that John and James requested.

We can get a sense of how and when and why we ask Jesus to do something for us by looking at our liturgical worship. After offering the Prayers of the People in the celebration of the Eucharist, the priest concludes all the petitions and intercessions that have been offered with a collect. Note a few of these and the tenor or the tone of those prayers.

"Lord, hear the prayers of your people; and what we have asked faithfully, grant that we may obtain effectually, to the glory of your name; through Jesus Christ our Lord."

"Heavenly Father, you have promised to hear what we ask in the Name of your Son: Accept and fulfill our petitions, we pray, not as we ask in our ignorance, nor as we deserve in our sinfulness, but as you know and love us in your Son Jesus Christ our Lord."

"Almighty God, to whom our needs are known before we ask: Help us to ask only what accords with your will; and those good things which we dare not, or in our blindness cannot ask, grant us for the sake of you Son Jesus Christ our Lord."

"What do you want me to do for you?" That's the question Jesus asked the brothers John and James. That's the question he asks us from time to time. Are we asking for the luxurious or the frivolous? Are we asking for the sustenance for our lives? Are we asking to be made well?

When I administer Unction, the Sacrament of Healing, most often I pray, in part, for persons in this way: "According to your will for this person, grant him or her healing in body, mind, or spirit." A major characteristic of Christians is that they put others ahead of themselves. Jesus was the great paradigm in that regard.

Finally, what is the adage? "Be careful what you ask for."

In *Children's Letters to God*, Joyce wrote the following:

"Dear God, Thank you for the baby brother,
but what I prayed for was a puppy."

The blind man wanted to see, and Jesus granted him that request. I wrote a meditation a few years ago about the possible consequences of someone having been made well who previously had been ill for 38 years. I noted that now that person will be expected to do certain things that he was unable to do previously like work, for example. No longer can the sick man expect others to furnish him money for his needs or assist him physically. Having gotten his health restored, society now has certain expectations.

All that aside, one thing has been made perfectly clear. That is that our God is in the business of hearing our prayers and granting them. Jesus told his followers that God will grant whatever we ask in Jesus' name. I can only imagine that John and James had an inkling of that reality for they were moved to approach Jesus who responded by asking them, "What do you want me to do for you?"

Meditation on a Question found in Genesis 17:17-21

"Shall a child be born to a man who is a hundred years old? Shall Sarah, who is ninety years old, bear a child?"

Immediately we can comprehend the questions that Abraham raised. Heck, we are amazed in this day and age when we hear about 50-year-old women giving birth to children. But ninety years old? Come on. We do not marvel too much at a man having children in his old age, what with people like Tony Randall and Larry King. But who imagines that a ninety-year-old woman is even remotely interested in matters of the birds and the bees or actually engaging in such related activities?

My initial thought after reading these questions and preparing to compose this meditation was "Suppose the trailblazers of our human existence had considered so many things to be impossibilities and failed to act on their dreams or their curiosity?" Surely man cannot fly. Why would anyone even consider that possibility? He does not have wings. Aerodynamically, he is not built for flight. So why even think about that possibility? Perhaps someone took a look at the bumblebee. I am told that from the physical point of view, that insect should not be able to fly. But he does. A now extinct

55555555555555

airline coined the phrase, "The Wings of Man." That echoes a great truth. Humans have landed on the moon, learning that it is not made of green cheese. Routinely now, jaunts to outer space occur. We can fly.

One of the greatest achievements in the history of our existence is the splitting of the atom. Of course, that has been a double-edged sword. With atomic power, we have the potential for generating cheap, long-term, inexhaustible energy to provide for the needs of people all over the world. But, we cannot forget Hiroshima and Nagasaki, Japan. What was done there is the darkside of the accomplishment of splitting the atom. By the same token, it was the nuclear weapons that ended the cold war. Both major super powers of the time came to the realization that there could not be a winner in a nuclear war. Creation and stockpiling of such weapons eventually showed the folly of contemplating use of such weapons of mass destruction. A double-edged sword indeed!

I am not clear at all about the most recent accomplishment of scientists, i.e., the cracking of the Human Genome code. It apparently has something to do with life. It has something to do with the mapping of the 30,000+ human genes and rendered them accessible for further study and manipulation. This, apparently, was a major accomplishment, which in previous times was considered an impossibility.

Citing the extraordinary is one way to look at Abraham's questions, but we don't have to venture off that far. We can simply look at everyday, ordinary events and products in our world. Some of us casually get into our automobiles and travel hundreds of miles to see relatives and friends, to attend business meetings, or simply to go on vacation. And we do so in the utmost of comfort: air conditioning or heating according to the outside temperature. Who in Abraham's day could have imagined that people could move from Point A to Point B in an enclosed vehicle without the benefit of animal power (or human power)? Indeed, who prior to the Industrial Revolution would have imagined that?

No meditation of mine would be complete without words from one of the little ones who composed letters for the book *Children's Letters to God*. Here is one that speaks to our discussion about impossibilities.

Dear God,
I bet it is
very hard
for you to
love all of
everybody in the whole world
There are only
4 people in our
family and I
can never do it.

Nan

Humans have been inventive. We cannot, however, say that this is all by man's doings. Humans have been graced with memory, reason, and skill by their Creator. We have been given dominion over all the earth, its animals and its resources. What we have accomplished we have done so because our God has given us the wherewithal to accomplish these things. These are gifts of God for the people of God.

I love the adage or quote—not sure which—that says, "We'll do the difficult today; the impossible will take a little longer." Humans dream. They consider all things possible. We have grown considerably from the times of Abraham. We also have been given a revelation of God through his only Son, Jesus. This Son of God reminded us that with God all things are possible. In Mark's gospel, this is clearly laid out for us. "Then Jesus looked around and said to his disciples, 'How hard it will be for those who have wealth to enter the kingdom of God.' And the disciples were perplexed at these words. But Jesus said to them again, 'Children, how hard it is to enter the kingdom of God! It is easier for a camel to go through the eye of a needle than for someone who is rich to enter the kingdom of God.' They were greatly astounded and said to one another, 'Then who can be saved?' Jesus looked at them and said, 'For mortals it is impossible, but not for God; for God all things are possible.'" (10:23-27)

The existence of so many impossible things and the execution of so many impossible tasks underscore the reality of how very possible is the impossible. The birth of a son to Abraham, who himself was old, and his old wife, Sarah, also underscores how possible the impossible is when God is the activating agent. That point is the key, I believe. Not in our own strength, but in yours, O Lord. Manna from heaven; the parting of the sea to provide safe passage for the Israelites, the Virgin birth; the feeding of the 5,000 with a mere sack lunch, the raising of Lazarus from the dead as the basis: these are all examples of impossibilities that became possibles in our human existence by the hands of and through the grace of God.

There is one impossibility that I hope to see in my lifetime. Look around the world and what one devastating occurrence is evident? War. Yes war, physical strife is a way of life for so many. Just very recently, hostilities broke out in the little nation of Haiti. Of course, our nation has completely overturned the Iraqi society, and daily we hear of bombings in that country. We also have troops fighting the Talibans in Afghanistan. These represent just the tip of the iceberg. I hope one day that I will see the impossible come to fruition: peace breaking out all over the world. Humans rationalize, and the thought of world peace can hardly be visualized by many. However, we have a great truth that "For God all things are possible." Abraham fathered a child by his ninety-year-old wife. That very ancient occurrence gives me hope that the impossible really can become reality and possible. I put my trust in God to make it happen.

Meditation on a Question found in Psalm 8

"What is man that you think of him, mere man that you care for him?"

Do I detect a lack of self-esteem in the psalmist here? He seems to be perplexed that God cares for him. He paints a picture supportive of my question. The psalmist is amazed that God has done so many things for humankind. He says that in spite of the lowliness of humanity, God has put humans in a certain position that is only a little lower than the angels. God has given humans stewardship over all that he has made: sheep and cattle and wilds animals too; the birds and fish and all the creatures in the seas.

"Why have you done this?" is the question about God that the psalmist ponders in this psalm.

Some of this humility ought to be available for some individuals I know. They think very highly of themselves indeed. I realize that is judgmental, and if you had known my wife when we were in high school, you would have known that she thought I was conceited and held that I too thought too highly of myself. We are people who would sort of expect God to do something for us. At least we'd not be intrigued that he was so gracious towards us.

There is a happy medium between the position of the psalmist and those who purportedly think so highly of themselves. There the truth about humankind lies.

The creation story offers some insight here. The first chapter chronicles the creation of heaven and earth, the moon, stars, plants, animals, and humankind. Of course humans were created in God's image; they were created male and female. They were given dominion over all things. And following the completion of the creation "God saw everything that he had made, and indeed, it was very good." Genesis 1:31. Note that the creation was not seen as just good but very good. Man and woman being included in that, we'd have to ask ourselves why the psalmist questioned as he did. Seemingly, it is fitting that God would do so much for humans.

Of course, in the fullness of time, God entered our history in a unique way. He took on the body and nature of humans becoming one of us. He did so to take our sins upon his own shoulders. He did so to author our salvation. He did so that we might become all that God intended us to be. I am captivated by the idea that God loved the body so much that he had to have one. (Or something to that effect)

I have often said that Jesus points the way to what it really means to be human. So to say, I'm just human is a cop out. Jesus our great paradigm shows us the potential and possibility of humanity. Being human is not just a matter of being flawed to the extent that we are unworthy, though we are that. Being human is a state of having been created in the very image of God. That speaks volumes, doesn't it? Jesus himself speaks about the possibility that humans can attain. Remember how he exhorted his followers—and consequently us—to be perfect as our Father in heaven is perfect. Would he have made such a statement if it were impossible to be perfect? We exist in a position that by the psalmist's admission is but just a little lower than the angels.

The gospel of John is famous for its message for every man and woman. For God so loved the world that he gave his only son that all who believe in him might not perish but have eternal life. For God sent his son into the world not to condemn the world but that the world might be saved by him. That says to me that God really has a great regard for his creatures. That says to me that people are special to God. Does the phase 'apple of his eye' come to mind?

After the Flood, God created the rainbow to be a symbol for us, to let us know that never again would he destroy life by water. The bow in the sky is the sign for both God and man of the promise that God has made to his people. Surely this is reflective of God's regard for us.

God gave the Law to his people through Moses the lawgiver. He opened the sea so that the Israelites might flee the pursuing Egyptians. He rained down manna from heaven so the people could eat the food of angels. He made the Jewish people to be a light unto the nations so that we might see and comprehend his love for us. And in the fullness of time, God sent his son to us. This Son, faithful to the Father all the way to the cross, demonstrates in a mighty way in what regard we are held in God's mind.

What is man that you think of him, mere man that you care for him? Indeed! It is a question that need not be posed or asked.

I remember studying a period in world literature called the Romantic period. The overriding characteristic of that period is the belief in the goodness of man. We learned it this way: "Man is basically good." How could that be far from the truth? After all, man was made in the image of God. Woman was made in the image of God. God is love, and God is good. It follows, doesn't it?

In baptism, we speak about seeking and serving Christ in others. Actually, this is one of the promises we make. My wife often observes that Christ is in each of us. Sometimes, however, we may need to dig a little deeper in some of us to find that Christ. But given that Christ is in us, there is good cause to make conclusions about the state of humans. What is man that you think of him? Indeed. What is man that you care for him? The psalmist should have known; and perhaps he did. Perhaps this is one of those rhetorical questions.

The good news is that for us who have fallen, for us who miss the mark from time to time, God has effected a remedy. Jesus in his earthly ministry urged his listeners to repent and believe the good news. Flawed. Yes we are that at times, but Jesus has provided a way for amendment of life.

For me the ultimate statement about how God regards us is found in one of the psalms—the 23rd.

The Lord is my shepherd, I shall not be in want.

He makes me to lie down in green pastures and leads me beside still waters.

He revives my soul and guides me along the pathways for his Name's sake.

Though I walk through the valley of the shadow of death, I shall fear no evil; for you are with me; your rod and your staff, they comfort me.

You spread a table before me in the presence of those who trouble me; you have anointed my head with oil, and my cup is running over.

Surely goodness and mercy shall follow me all the days of my life, and I will dwell in the house of the Lord for ever.

Perhaps the psalmist's question was in the same vein as the title of a great hymn, "What wondrous love is this?" Indeed, God thinks of us; he cares for us. Man is the most important thing in the entire created world to God. What is man that he thinks of us, mere man that he cares for us? We are nothing less than the apple of his eye, the creatures that are able to reciprocate the love he shares with us. And we are the creatures that can do so voluntarily. We do not have to be coerced to love God. As it is his nature to love us, so it is ours to return that love.

Meditation on a Question found in Mark 8:27-30

"But who do you say that I am?"

One Saturday in the recent past, one of the cable television stations ran various marathons of some old TV programs. One of those was the adventures of the Lone Ranger, of which I have been a fan since the 1950s. I watched as many episodes as I could, and I recorded as many of these half-hour programs as I could on videotapes. The plot of all these stories is the same as I analyze them. There is some trouble in some territory; the Lone Ranger and his faithful companion, Tonto, ride in and save the day. At the end of the show, the masked man rides out of town shouting, while some who never knew who the man was asks, "Who was that masked man?" Of course, the standard answer is, "Why he's the Lone Ranger." That is so predictable.

Jesus, like the Lone Ranger, has come into town, and he has made waves by what he has done and by what he has said. He has preached with authority; not like previous holy men. He has preached a new message. He has spoken about God in intimate terms. He has healed the sick; raised the dead; and performed countless signs and miracles. He has put himself on a plane adjacent with God. In some people's vernacular, he has upset the apple cart. The Jewish officials are up in arms about the thoughts, words, and deeds of this man.

Jesus knows how he is perceived among the people, both the clergy of the day and the lay persons. But just as in business we like to have scorecards of how our products or our services are being received, so too Jesus was concerned about his message—the kingdom of heaven is at hand; repent and receive the good news! Jesus depended on the men he had assembled to travel and work with him—his disciples—to be his eyes and ears. So he inquired of them about the effectiveness of his ministry. Jesus asked them first about who the people say that he is. And, you remember all the various answers he was given. Clearly the people recognized Jesus as "something else" because they assigned various lofty names to him. The suggestion that he might be one of the ancient prophets. The name John the Baptist was one answer; Elijah was another. Seemingly Jesus expected such answers from the populace.

Then Jesus turned to those closest to him; those he had called; those who had left wife and brother and sister and family and jobs to follow him; those who had accepted the challenge to fish for people; those who ate, drank, and slept with him; those who traveled the dusty roads from town to town with him; and those who ministered with him, hearing his sermons and teachings and witnessing his miracles. Being so very close to him, Jesus must have been very curious about how his close companions viewed him. So he said, "But who do you say that I am?"

The identity of a person or an entity seems to be quite important to people. For example, when Moses was approached by God to assist in freeing the People of Israel from bondage in Egypt, Moses asked God to tell him who he should say that God is. Apparently those people needed such validation or information.

On the night Jesus was betrayed, he told his disciples that one of them would do the unspeakable deed. The disciples, in turn, asked the Master, "Lord, is it I?"

Biblically, Pilate asks Jesus if he is the King of the Jews. Franco Zeffirelli in his movie, *Jesus of Nazareth*, and taking some poetic license, has Pilate asking Jesus, "Who are you? What are you?"

Saul, on his way to Damascus to incarcerate men of the Way (as Christians were known then), was blinded by a great light. And he heard a voice ask him why he persecuted him. Saul responded, "Who are you Lord?" Acts 9:5

I have been involved in many workshops where the moderator or facilitator uses an icebreaker that involves each participant telling something about himself so that the group will know or have some sense of whom each of us is.

The identity of a person is a key piece of information in the intercourse of people. Knowing with whom one is dealing is vital. A major, Eastern Insurance Underwriter, Chubb and Son, for whom I worked 3 years, required its underwriters to travel to visit face-to-face with the agents that represented them so that the underwriters would know who the players were.

Finally, consider all that we do in this world, privately or corporately, that have some goal, some aim, or some bottomline. There needs to be some way to measure the results, the effectiveness, and the bottomline. Jesus had done much in his day. He had even caused some to oppose him.

The people during Jesus' time were expecting the promised messiah. They felt the time for his appearance was imminent. That, however, in all likelihood, had been complicated by the appearance of false messiahs. So in view of the religious officials' strict requirements to the Law, in view of the political climate of the day, the people may have been confused, reticent, or downright skeptical about any prophets or preachers regardless of their words and deeds. I think it was in that context that Jesus posed his initial question to his disciples.

In this modern age, we have the benefit of the Word in so many languages. Our salvation history has been read and studied in so many places at so many times. We know Jesus from the Bible, which has been translated broadly. We do have a cloud of witnesses in the written word. Preachers have been vocal over the centuries, and so very many of us have heard their sermons and homilies about Jesus. We recognize the real presence of Christ in the Eucharist which we partake on a weekly basis in the main. We cannot explain it, but somehow Jesus is present for us in the breaking of the bread and in the prayers. This Jesus, too, is present in all people.

Given all the knowledge we have at our disposal, given the revelation, given the intimacy in the sacraments, we really should be assured about the identity of Jesus. Right? Of course, we know how those early disciples answered Jesus' question about who they say he is. And we know that it was our man

Peter who, inspired by the Holy Spirit, got the correct answer. Peter told Jesus "You are the messiah." Mark 8:29

If we are to be effective followers of Jesus in this age, then we have to be crystal clear about the identity of Jesus. The question Jesus posed was not meant just for Peter and John and James and the others. No, that question accrues to us in this day. Is it enough for us to parrot Peter and say that Jesus is the messiah? What does that mean? Messiah. What does that mean to the average person today? Can't we put our own perspective on the answer? I am sure Jesus is seeking a personalized response. So given all the answers that have been offered over the centuries and the knowledge and experiences we now have, Jesus says to us, "But who do you say that I am?"

Meditation on a Question found in John 18:33-38

Pilate said to him, "What is truth?"

This has to be one of the all-time great questions. Just three little words, but how many of us can answer the question satisfactorily? How much time and space would it take to adequately answer the question? What is truth?

I guess I should begin by taking a crack at an answer. Succinctly, why couldn't we say that truth is the absence of error? Or perhaps we could say that truth is reality uncovered, unmasked, or unclouded by human rationale and apologies. I am not even sure I am clear about what I just wrote. But most people would agree that truth is the other side of falsehood.

Perhaps the only way we can answer Pilate's question is to ask more questions and to say of what truth is the opposite.

Truth is now what I am hearing could have saved Martha Stewart from her current plight. So many critics have suggested that things would have been different for the former domestic diva if only she had come clean, i.e., if she had told the truth.

Bill Clinton the former two-term president of the United States was impeached because he did not come forth initially with the truth. Most critics now say that he could have avoided that ordeal. He could have saved the country from the trial if only he had told the truth about his relation with a former aide.

These two examples make a well-known adage a reality. "The truth will set you free."

So, it seems that whatever truth is, it is something that we ought not to keep to ourselves. Truth seems to be something that most people are willing to accept. Would Pontius Pilate have done differently had Jesus given him truth? Would history have been different if Jesus had been forthcoming with the truth? What might Pilate have done if Jesus had explained exactly what is meant by truth? We'll never know now.

The poet attempted to give us insight as to the matter of truth. Remember how he wrote "Beauty is truth, truth beauty. That's all ye know on earth and all ye need know." Now we have introduced another element on the other side of the equation for truth. But this is not relevant. Look at the context of Pilate's question. Jesus told Pilate that he had come into the world to speak about the truth. That's what led Pilate to ask the now famous question.

Truth cannot be that illusive, can it? When a mother questions a child about an incident or some accident, she exhorts him to tell her the truth! In such context, truth seems to be the relating of facts about an event or happening in such a way that the unadorned disclosure is what is offered. As best as the person can relay it, the story is told as it actually happened.

In other words, if the matter had been videotaped, there would be no deviation between the story told and the event as viewed on the videotape.

Ah! We're getting somewhere now. Truth is fact that is not embellished, fact that mirrors unfallen creation. God's word is truth. Who, then, is in a position to give the truth?

For grins, I browsed the internet using the monosyllabic "truth" in my search engine. Guess what I found? I found more articles than you can imagine about truth in some form, shape, or fashion. But it was the remarks of a United States Senator that caught my attention. Here I printed the preamble or opening statement only. To wit,

Truth has a way of asserting itself despite all attempts to obscure it. Distortion only serves to derail it for a time. No matter to what lengths we humans may go to obfuscate facts or delude our fellows, truth has a way of squeezing out through the cracks, eventually. But the danger is that at some point it may no longer matter. The danger is that damage is done before the truth is widely realized. The reality is that, sometimes, it is easier to ignore uncomfortable facts and go along with whatever distortion is currently in vogue.
Senator Robert C. Byrd, Senate Floor Remarks, May 21, 2003.

Pilate went along with a distortion. He knew that Jesus was not guilty of anything substantive. But as Byrd said, it was easier to go along with what is not true. I am no longer dumbfounded that Pilate asked the question, His very actions gave him away.

RICHARD EDWIN CRAIG, III

My little kids had something to say on the matter of truth. Hear their words. [*From Children's Letters to God*]

"Dear GOD, My brother told me about being born but it doesn't sound right. They're just kidding, aren't they? – Marsha"

"Dear GOD, We read Thomas Edison made light. But in Sunday school they said You did it. So I bet he stoled your idea. Sincerely, Donna"

"Dear GOD, Please send me a pony. I never asked for anything before, You can look it up. –Bruce"

And so it goes...

Despite all we have heard this day, truth seems to be an elusive entity. It is not quite like nailing Jell-O to the wall, but there can be variants to truth. How can that be and still have truth? Ever hear or read about those experiments that have been conducted about eye-witness accounts and testimonies? Take 10 people witnessing an event; ask them to describe what happened. It would be rare—darn near impossible—to get ten stories that meshed in all details. And since all witnessed the event, we have to conclude that what gets relayed by these persons is truth.

In the same way we know the story about the blind persons who were permitted to hold onto a different part of an elephant like the trunk and the tail and the leg and the ear, and the like. You know how the description of an elephant differed among those in this group.

With that in mind consider how in a court of law we make people lay their hands on the Bible and swear that they will tell the truth and nothing but the truth.

It doesn't get any easier. Jesus who evoked Pilate to ask this question about truth had something to say about truth prior to the time he was put on trail. Jesus told his disciples that they knew the way to the place where he was going to prepare a place for them. When they voiced that they might not know, Jesus declared that he was the "way, the truth, and the life." Wait a minute here. Why didn't Jesus tell Pilate this?

Earlier when the Jewish officials questioned Jesus, he said to them he would not tell them whether he was the Messiah because they would not believe him (Luke 22:66-69). Gives credence to the adage, "Some people just don't want to hear the truth."

All this boils down to something basic and simple I think. From the *Merriam-Webster Online Dictionary*, we find these definitions:

1 a archaic: FIDELITY, CONSTANCY b: sincerity in action, character, and utterance

2 a (1): the state of being the case: FACT (2): the body of real things, events, and facts: ACTUALITY (3) often capitalized: a transcendent fundamental or spiritual reality b: a judgment, proposition, or idea that is true or accepted as true <truths of thermodynamics> c: the body of true statements and propositions

3 a: the property (as of a statement) of being in accord with fact or reality b chiefly British: TRUE 2 c: fidelity to an original or to a standard

The one that caught my eye is truth being "a transcendent fundamental or spiritual reality." If Jesus had used that as his response to Pilate, history and the gospel writers would have recorded the shortest verse in the Bible. Pilate would have said, "Huh?"

"What is truth?" Jesus was asked. He did not feel compelled to answer that question and neither do I.

Meditation on a Question found in John 1:43-51

"Can anything good come out of Nazareth?"

It is amazing how humans create their own images and thoughts about people and places. Mention to some people the Summit Restaurant in Racine, and immediately there is a perception about the kind of restaurant it is. What images are generated when you hear the name Tacos El Rey? I don't really know, but I would wager some serious cash that the perception would not be as high as it is for the former restaurant mentioned.

The arts are very big in this city. I personally have never encountered so many people who enjoy and patronize the arts, particularly the opera. So what do people in this town think about Outkast? Or Herbie Hancock?

Recent discussions about moving schools and programs in the Racine Unified School District made it perfectly clear to me that some felt there was something less than desirable in the latest flagship of that district. I speak of the Julian Thomas School. I heard one woman testifying that she did not want her children to go to school "with those people."

Have you ever heard the question—or something akin to it—like, "Well, what can you expect from those people?"

A certain attitude of superiority is evident in certain segments of society. Most often it has to do with, or it is centered in, wealth. Sometimes it is centered on breeding. Can I say "breeding?" It was centered on culture.

There was an Episcopal parish in a small, working class community, which is an oddity in itself. Typically one finds some wealthy parishioners—at least those who are well off—in Episcopal churches. This parish may have had one person who fell into such categories of wealth.

Celebrations often are characterized by little tea sandwiches, which had the crust on the bread cut off. Not so with that parish. Such things were apparently not necessary. That speaks to how different people "process or present." Functional rather than elegant was the hallmark of those members.

My wife had an aunt who was a very judgmental person. She was a status hound. She liked to rub elbows with all the right people. She looked askance at certain people. One of her favorite creeds was "An apple doesn't fall far from the tree." I can see how this may not be a bad thing necessarily; however, this woman meant it in its negative connotation. This woman certainly held very specific thoughts about certain people. They just didn't come up to her standards.

My mother should have been born on the other side of the tracks. She had those rich tastes, and her son (who is writing this) inherited the gene that creates those tastes as well. A kid accused one of my sons and his whole family of being snobs. I recall the family "discussions during my childhood." So many times my mother would tell my dad who was doing what. For example, she'd say something like, "The Scotts are doing this; the Alexanders are going to the event," and the like. Keep in mind those families were in the wealthier stratus of society. My family was not. But my mother had an idea of what the upper crust did, wore, ate, and the like. And she attempted to influence my father in such a way that we would do certain of those things the other group did.

We all know the Christmas story, which tells us about the birth of Jesus in a stable or a cave. He was not born in Northside Hospital in Atlanta, Georgia as our boys were; he was not even born in the hospital at the All Saints' complex in Racine. He did not have attending physicians and nurses. There were no rooms: either private or semi-private. He was lucky to have been born in a stable.

The family fled to Egypt where they stayed for a time. Then when they felt the danger to the child had passed, they moved to Nazareth where Jesus grew up and everyone came to know him as the son of Joseph. Remember how he made a declaration following his reading of scripture in his hometown synagogue? It was then they put him into context by speaking of his lineage.

Jesus' parents were not well educated, it seems—at least not in the formal sense. His father, Joseph, was a carpenter. No doubt that profession was such that the father probably had a good income. But that was not like being those authorities who loved to go about in long robes and who were recognized by the people. Mary, his mother, was a virgin. She was extremely young when Jesus was born. It is doubtful that she, like most women of her day, had any formal education.

So Jesus grew up in that context. We know very little about Jesus' childhood and development. We often call him a carpenter. There is some speculation in academic circles that Jesus did spend some time in the community of the Essenes, and it was there he was educated. We have no definitive proof of that however.

Nazareth was probably like many very small American towns. Not much is to be found in such little communities. Here I speak about things like businesses employing large numbers of people, home or regional offices of major businesses, industries, and the like. Simple folk is what one is most likely to find in small places. Except for the eccentric, one is not likely to find wealth or the cultured in such places.

Even when Jesus set out on his earthly ministry, he presented an image of an itinerate preacher. He walked everywhere he went. The upper crust had carriages born by humans and possibly by animals in some cases. He seemingly wore simple clothing. He looked like anything but a king. He was not adorned lavishly or otherwise with jewelry or other signature pieces of rank. People naturally generate a certain perception of such a person.

Philip told Nathanael that they had found the person who was spoken of by Moses and by the prophets. This man was the one to fulfill all the promises. Nathanael, no doubt, had his own ideas about the résumé of the one who would fulfill all the law and the prophets. Jesus, apparently, did not fill the bill. No doubt Nathanael was very familiar with Nazareth. He obviously did not hold that town and its inhabitants in very high regard. And so to Philip, Nathanael put forth an almost rhetorical question. He asked Philip, "Can anything good come out of Nazareth?" It was left to Jesus himself to persuade Nathanael that a persons' birthplace, or his hometown residence should not be tenets that govern how we look at people. In the same way, the side of the tracks should not be the determining factor. Nathanael, in a direct interaction with Jesus, came to understand the identity of the man.

Hopefully as we interact with different persons in this day, and as we seek to serve Christ in all people, we will not use false criteria to accept or to reject people. Hopefully we can come to grips with the truth, which is that something good can come out of Nazareth, Racine, Aransas Pass, Chicago, New York City, and any other place where people are willing to live out their faith in Christ Jesus. Yes Nathanael, something good did come out of that place.

Meditation on a Question found in Genesis 29:1-14

"Do you know Laban the son of Nahor?"

People are always trying to 'hook up' by showing some kind of relationship. I use the term 'hook up' because it is in the vernacular of the young people of this day, and it really gets across the idea I express here. Hook up is a task that involves letting someone else know how another person is related to the both of us. It is something we do all the time.

In business, we do not hesitate to drop a name that lets a person know that we know someone the person also knows. In the life insurance business, agents always ask for leads, i.e., names of persons a customer knows. When an agent calls on those leads, he uses that person's name, and surprisingly, just that reference opens many doors. It takes a call out of the 'cold call' arena, and warms up a potential client. It is amazing how that works.

Jacob had traveled some distance, and he needed to get in touch with his kinsman. So he threw out the name to see how it played out. "Do you know Laban the son of Nahor?" A well-placed question can do wonders.

Once upon a time, I took it upon myself to write an open letter to a church in Atlanta, Georgia. That church was in the midst of some turmoil because of a change to their clergy leadership. The pastor was a man who was very charismatic. He was a national figure, and very well respected in the human rights field. He was, no doubt, a spiritual man. And the congregation was up in arms because his bishop had moved him to another church. That's how deployment changes were handled in the Methodist Church at that time.

As a result of the move of the pastor, some in the congregation had felt a need to regroup in a number of areas. A capital funds or building funds drive was put on hold—perhaps suspended indefinitely. Some people had begun considering moving to the other church, which was in the same city, to be with that minister.

This is the backdrop to a sticky situation in the church in which I was born and raised. My mother had been a 50-year member of that church. All my siblings attended that church as well. We had much history there. I left that church only because I followed my beloved to the Episcopal Church.

However, when my mother told me about the things taking place there, I felt moved by the Spirit to write an open letter to the members of that church; to help them understand what it is that God calls us to; to remind them on whom our focus should rest: Jesus.

So I composed this letter to do just that. But I knew that there might be those who had forgotten me. There might be those who came to that church following my departure, and they would not know me. There might be those who would need a reintroduction. So the first part of my epistle was spent telling the people who I was. I spent that time hooking up—I dropped names of persons who were previously and who were still at that time influential persons in the life of that church. I needed them to listen to what I believed God was leading me to say to them. I did not need them to dismiss me because I was an unknown quantity.

So in effect, I used the same tactic employed by Jacob. I asked that congregation if they knew Mrs. Mitchell, everyone's first Sunday school teacher. I asked them if they remembered those little chairs, in which we sat around that little table, where she told us that Jesus loves us. I asked them if they remembered this person and that person, using those names skillfully and strategically so that the hearers and the readers of my letter would be convinced that I was no mere outsider; so that they would understand that I was not a stranger to that church; and finally so that they would understand that in truth I was really one of them though I was separated by physical distance and the tenets of a different Expression (i.e., denomination).

The Good News is that it worked. The people knew the persons to whom I referred. The minister even followed my exhortation and made my letter available by reading it at the sermon time. Xerox copies of my letter were subsequently made and distributed to a large number of the faithful of that church.

It was all about hooking up. It was all about drawing lines between commonalties of various peoples to make their linkages apparent.

When we talk about the kinds of prayer, we learn that one particular kind is the intercessory prayer. "Intercession, [simply] brings before God the needs of others." *Book of Common Prayer* 857 On Sundays, our prayers are almost all prayers of intercession. How often have we asked others to "pray for me?"

One of the great intercessors in our faith is Mary, the Virgin. Mary is not the one who grants any petitions; what she does is influences the outcome. My kids learned very early that I love my wife very much, and I will do anything for her. So when they wanted something from me, they went to her, recognizing that their chances of getting their request would be greater if she was the one who asked. That is hooking up.

Our Lord Jesus demonstrated that this is a tactic that we can take and be successful in certain of our relations with God the Father. What did he say to his disciples and to us about the things for which we ask? Jesus told us that God will grant us whatever we ask of him when we ask for it in the name of Jesus. In fact, the catechism defines Christian prayer in the following way: "Christian prayer is response to God the Father, through Jesus Christ, in the power of the Holy Spirit." That's a form of hooking up.

Jacob had traveled a great distance to the land of his relative. He asked a question as much for direction as anything else. However, he knew that the particular question would open doors for him as well. Jacob asked a group of men where they lived. When they told him Haran, the home of his relative, he asked them, "Do you know Laban the son of Nahor?"

Meditation on a Question found in Exodus 4:1-12

"Who has made man's mouth? Who makes him dumb, or deaf, or seeing, or blind? Is it not I, the Lord?"

In this interchange between Moses and God, Moses seems to offer one excuse after another. Isn't that what we all do when we don't want to do something? Well I would, but...

Moses tells God about his speech impediment. He is not able to converse very well. He says that he is "slow of speech and tongue." That would have done it for me, but not God. That's when God asks his questions: "Who has made man's mouth? Who makes him dumb, or deaf, or seeing, or blind? Is it not I, the Lord?"

To drive to Walt Disney World in Orlando, Florida from San Antonio, Texas, it is necessary to drive over the Mississippi River Bridge at Baton Rouge. In 1977 when I relocated to Texas, I saw this bridge for the very first time, and quite frankly, it was intimidating. The way they make you approach the bridge, you do not know you are going to have to cross it until you are at the foot of the bridge. It is, I guess, a suspension bridge—there are no posts, pillars or other means of support beneath the bridge. It has these massive girders overhead. At its highest point, ships below appear miniature. Man figured out the science and the mathematics of constructing this magnificent structure. I am still in awe simply trying to contemplate how they did it for there is no way they could have used scaffolding or other structures to aid in the construction.

I have never gone atop the Empire State Building, which once upon a time was the tallest building in this country. I stood at the foot of that building in the 1960s, and I watched it and the other skyscrapers in New York City sway. Yes, they move. I understand they build them that way because if they were not able to do so, i.e., move, then they would break and like Jill come tumbling down.

We know that based on the lack of aerodynamic perfection, the bumblebee should not be able to fly. Man does not even have wings. Who would have ever thought that one day travel in the air from one place on this earth to another would be a routine occurrence? Until the retirement of that marvelous 'bird' called the Concorde, travel to Europe for commercial passengers was a mere three hours. It used to take me that long to travel from San Antonio to my hometown, Atlanta, Georgia. In the beginning, there was trial and error, but the Wright brothers put the primitive knowledge together to produce the first flight of humans. Of course, now outer space is within our reach.

I remember in the 1950s that we were given a drop that was supposed to make us immune to a disease called Polio. My friend Earl had an older sister named Griselda, and she had polio. Throughout my childhood, I recall a few others stricken with this disease. But polio was declared eradicated in the past because of the work of Jonah Salk and others who pioneered the creation of an immunization.

Wonderful things in other areas have been wrought. I think of all the writers who have put pen to paper and created beautiful, powerful works of prose and poetry. I think of William Shakespeare, John Donne, Niki Giovanni, and John Grisham. I think I have written some good things myself. I have four unpublished volumes of poetry that I have written over the past years. Some of what I wrote is noteworthy.

But how have humans been able to exploit the universe? How have humans been able to uncover and discover the secrets of the universe? Are Physics and Chemistry innate disciplines within the race? What made us want to put words on paper and record things, like our thoughts, our convictions, our history, and the like?

If we accept the big bang theory of creation, then we can say these things are mere accident. Fortuitous is the word that describes this possibility for me. Just out of the blue, man gets an inkling that he can solve some problem. In fact, out of the blue he gets an idea that there is a problem or challenge to be addressed. For me, that simply does not sit well.

We know that in the beginning God created the heavens and the earth, all things that are seen and all things that remain unseen. He created life, and among that life is humankind. Christians understand that in that creation action, God granted in his creatures memory, reason, and skill. He made us in the image of God, which we most often talk about in the context of being "free to make choices: to love, to create, to reason, and to live in harmony with creation and with God." *The Book of Common Prayer* 845

For us who are Christians, we have a revelation of God in the person of Jesus of Nazareth. Jesus being the mirror image of God the Father, we have come to understand much more than we ever knew about the creative force in the world. This Jesus said one thing that is very interesting relative to this discussion. He told his disciples that they would do even greater things. This was in reference to himself and all the things he had done.

Moses is one of those persons who had not gotten it right yet. He was approached by God to assist in the freeing of God's people who were held in captivity in Egypt. Moses no doubt thought about himself, his own personal limitations, his own weaknesses, his own deficiencies, and the like. Moses thought about going out to do the work that God had given him to do but in his own strength. That's the mistake so many people make in the world today, particularly in this country. There is too much emphasis on self-reliance. I have attempted to overcome this tendency in my own life in my morning prayers. One of my petitions is this: Grant O Lord that I may be in your strength and that your Holy Spirit will guide me if I encounter any who seek you or otherwise need your help."

The psalmist asked, "From where is my help to come?" And he answers, "My help comes from the Lord who made heaven and earth."

All of that, it seems, is the lesson God tried to impart to Moses. Sure, Moses had a speech impediment. Of course, he was not a Philadelphia lawyer and certainly was not eloquent in speech. Moses had pondered and suggested that he might not be the man for the job in view of his inadequacies.

Moses, the great Lawgiver, came on the scene just a little late to have known one major fact. Do you recall the time Jesus talked to his disciples about the near impossibility of a rich man getting into heaven? Do you remember how Jesus said it would be easier for a camel to go through an eye of a needle than for a rich man to get into heaven? So his disciples asked Jesus who, then, could be saved. Jesus told them that things which are impossible or which appear to be impossible are possible with God.

So I need not be amazed at all the "progress" that humans have brought about over the centuries. Airplanes and flight, mighty and magnificent structures, medicines and cures for diseases, the ability to read and write: all things and the ability to create them are wrought at the hands of God. It is curious that Moses who was quite intimate with God should have had such hesitancy. Moses was focusing on his own humanness and abilities. And that is why God brought to his attention the fact that speech and the ability to use it were possible because God made them possible. Not one thing was made that was not made through him—that's what John tells us in his prologue to his Gospel. It stands to reason that the person who made speech possible can enhance it so that the person can be persuasive and eloquent according to the needs.

Again, I need not be amazed at all the "progress" that humans have brought about over the centuries. All I have to do is to eavesdrop on that conversation between God and Moses and hear these questions once more. "Who has made man's mouth? Who makes him dumb, or deaf, or seeing, or blind? Is it not I, the Lord?"

Meditation on a Question found in Genesis 37:1-11

"What is this dream that you have dreamed? Shall I and your mother and your brothers indeed come to bow ourselves to the ground before you?"

The notes in the *Access Bible* have this to say. "The story about Jacob's son, Joseph, is the longest continuous narrative in Genesis. The Joseph story provides a fitting conclusion to the Genesis ancestor stories as the family grows larger to become the people or nation of Israel. The story also functions as a literary bridge to the events in Egypt in the book of Exodus. Joseph will be the first of the Israelites to be enslaved in Egypt and then rescued, a fate all Israel will eventually share." p. 50

This situation in which Joseph found himself reminds me of Cinderella. I guess in a way this is a classic version of the same story.

Joseph's brother's already hated him. That is no exaggeration—that fact is stated clearly in the beginning of the narrative. His father loved the young boy Joseph because he was the product of his old age. Jacob had even made a special coat for the lad.

Now in his teen years, a time when grandiosity can be apparent, Joseph had a dream. I am amazed by how those primitive people looked at things. The first reaction from Joseph's father about the dream was "What is this dream that you have dreamed?" It is as if Joseph—or anyone else for that matter—could have controlled what he dreamed. And then the crux of the matter: "Shall I and your mother and your brothers indeed come to bow ourselves to the ground before you?"

It is as if Joseph had gotten out of his place, as if he had forgotten his place. The brothers hated Joseph all the more. The father "kept the matter in mind."

In the Cinderella story, our girl got to attend the ball and literally had herself a ball. She partied with the prince and had simply a gay old time! Then the inevitable: she lost one of her slippers, which did not vanish at the stroke of midnight. It was the source of the identity of the person who wore it. The times when this story was written must have been like Hollywood—only one person in the entire kingdom could wear that particular slipper. That aside aside, the wicked stepmother and her daughters could not fathom that their Cinderella could fit into the slipper. They probably assumed the same attitude that Jacob and his boys took when Joseph told them about his dream.

That kind of attitude seems to have some recurrence in real life.

When I was sent on TDY to the Information Systems area for three years, I became familiar with the politics of the computer and technological ethos. During those years in the 1980s, a program, Pacbase, which was written in France, could generate code—the instructions that programmers write to make the computer do a task or multiple tasks—automatically. With Pacbase, all the programmers had to do was to place labels on the screens, which is where the user interacted with the program, and Pacbase would generate all the necessary code behind the screens to make them useful to the user community. This program, by the way, was called a fourth generation language.

No one could have been opposed to that program, right? Wrong! The person who uncovered or discovered this particular language was at odds with some in influential positions. They got hung up on who was introducing this program to the company rather than how beneficial the program would be to the company. "Shall I and your mother and your brothers indeed come to bow ourselves to the ground before you?" I heard that all over again in the twentieth century.

God uses the most unlikely persons to do those things:

Moses the man who was "slow of speech and tongue," to assist in freeing God's people held captive in Egypt; Gideon who questioned his abilities, and then went out to defeat the formidable Midianites; David to continue to be king even in the face of adultery and murder. Mary, an unwed, peasant girl who resided in an obscure village to become the God-bearer; Paul, formerly known as Saul, the Pharisee who pursued the people of the Way relentlessly and put many of them to death to introduce the Gentiles to Jesus; and Martin, a Baptist minister, to bring about civil rights for a large number of persons in our own country; God has his own ways of doing things. In Isaiah, this is made perfectly clear. "For my thoughts are not your thoughts, nor your ways my ways, says the Lord. For as the heavens are higher than the earth, so are my ways higher than your ways, and my thoughts than your thoughts."

For us who believe that Jesus of Nazareth is the Son of God, this man born to simple parents in a stable in an out of the way place, we have a perfect, real live example that God does things in a manner not contemplated by humans. Like so many who waited for the Lord, we might have had him be born to a family of nobility and probably in the greatest of luxury of the time, a palace perhaps. But again, that is not God's way.

Jacob loved his son, but Jacob obviously did not think that Joseph would rise to the point that he and his family would be subservient to Joseph. It was unimaginable. It was, to put it just a bit more bluntly, unthinkable!

But if one really considers the dream that Joseph experienced, it is difficult to conclude anything else. The family was right in their interpretation of Joseph's dreams.

Some of us who resided in Texas were amazed that George Bush, a fellow Texan, rose all the way to the presidency of this country.

Joseph had two dreams that seemed to indicate that Joseph would have a primordial position over his family. What they could not conceive was that the position would be over a nation as well. In one way, Jesus spoke about our modern day adage which holds that familiarity breeds contempt. Jesus said that a prophet is accepted everywhere except in his own hometown. Makes me wonder how successful I could be as a priest if I ministered among the people of Atlanta, Georgia. Isn't that the son of Richard, the Post Office letter carrier, and his wife Nettie Craig? Can he indeed lead us pastorally?

Who in our lives is in the position of Joseph? Have we missed out on some grace because the person was familiar to us? Likewise have we missed an opportunity because it meant being subordinate to one who was like Joseph in relationship to us? Has that pride been allowed to color our acceptance of someone important in our lives? Now is certainly a good time to examine our lives and our relationships to see if there are those we need to accept as our leaders, or our points of inspiration, and the like.

The reality is that we can never be sure who will command our allegiance from our standpoint as a subordinate. In every life, especially as we think more highly of ourselves than perhaps we ought to, there will be Josephs in our lives. God just has a knack of doing the unconventional. In time, we will see the justice in it.

Meditation on a Question found in Joel 2:12-16

"Who knows whether he will not turn and repent, and leave a blessing behind him, a cereal offering and a drink offering for the Lord, your God?"

Our God is a God of love and mercy, but he is also a God who has given us rules by which we are to abide. He has given us rules of life that we should assimilate into our lives. He has given us rules to mold and shape us to be the people he has created us to be. Throughout our salvation history, we have been reminded of this through prophets, judges, and others who have led the exhortation to righteous and holy living.

But throughout our salvation history, we have seen that our God can and does punish those who refuse to accept him and the ways he has set out for us.

When God looked early on at his creation, he found that the people had seriously separated themselves from him. *The Amplified Bible* puts it this way: "And God looked upon the world and saw how degenerate, debased, and vicious it was, for all humanity had corrupted their way upon the earth and lost their true direction." *Genesis 6:12* Because of this human condition, God told Noah that he intended to destroy these people and the land. God, as we know, followed through on this promise. The wicked of that time were utterly destroyed. But Noah and his family survived the flood to become the yeast for the continuation of human life.

When Lot was escaping the wrath of God brought to a sinful town, Lot was told not to look back. Lot's wife did not heed this warning, and she became as Morton Salt, a full pillar of it in fact.

Moses, the great Lawgiver, went up on the holy mountain to speak with God and to receive the commandments for living drafted by God for the people. In Moses' absence, the people did sin greatly. And as a result, a large number of those people, once saved from the jaws of enslavement, were destroyed. They made the wrong choice.

Those are just a few examples of how God followed through with his promise to punish those that sin and separate themselves from him, and who totally and willfully miss the mark. However, there is precedence in what Joel has suggested, i.e., that our sins may not bring our demise if we denounce our sinful ways. Joel tells us, "Who knows whether he will not turn and repent, and leave a blessing behind him, a cereal offering and a drink offering for the Lord, your God?"

King David, whom we accord the status of capital-S Saint, is an example of the duality of God's promise to punish and to save. Remember that David became involved with a married woman, Bathsheba, and he committed adultery. That was not sin enough for him, he also engineered the fatal demise of her husband, Uriah the Hittite, after his scheme to make Uriah think he may have fathered the child with which Bathsheba was now pregnant, was foiled. Nathan, the prophet, is the one who brought David up short. He told him a parable parallel to David's sin. When David came to understand that the sin was his, he repented. God forgave David, but his punishment was the loss of the child born to him and Bathsheba. The account in *2 Samuel* states this reality: The servants asked David why he fasted and then stopped upon learning that the child had died. David said, "While the child was still alive, I fasted and wept; for I said, 'Who knows? The LORD may be gracious to me, and the child may live.'" *12:22* That's the theme of this meditation. However, there are consequences at the same time there is forgiveness.

One of my favorite characters in the Bible is Jonah, whom God directed to go to Ninevah on two occasions to warn the people there of impending death and destruction if they did not turn from their sinful ways. Of course, we know that Jonah got sidetracked initially because he had his own agenda. But when he finally complied with the request of God, the people repented. The king of Ninevah and all the people repented. They fasted, put on sackcloth and ashes; they did not permit their livestock to eat. The king rationalized, "Who can tell, God may turn and revoke His sentence against us, and turn away from his fierce anger so that we perish not." *Jonah 3:9* Sound familiar? And yes, God did not punish as he had threatened. The people were spared because they met God's terms.

Psalm 103, I usually refer to as the Ash Wednesday psalm. In it is the good news of hope for us when we heed God's admonitions and return to the Lord. Hear those words of hope:

3 He forgives all your sins *
and heals all your infirmities;
4 He redeems your life from the grave *
and crowns you with mercy and loving-kindness;
7 He made his ways known to Moses *
and his works to the children of Israel.
8 The Lord is full of compassion and mercy, *
slow to anger and of great kindness.
9 He will not always accuse us, *
nor will he keep his anger for ever.
10 He has not dealt with us according to our sins, *
nor rewarded us according to our wickedness.
11 For as the heavens are high above the earth, *
so is his mercy great upon those who fear him.
12 As far as the east is from the west, *
so far has he removed our sins from us.
13 As a father cares for his children, *
so does the Lord care for those who fear him.
14 For he himself knows whereof we are made; *
he remembers that we are but dust.

The People of Israel expected a savior, one anointed of God, who would come and take away the sins of the world: the Lamb of God. For too many centuries humankind had proven itself unable to live as God had ordained. Humans needed some assistance; they needed more than had been previously provided to them. The Evangelist makes it clear how God looks upon us when he writes, "For God so loved the world that he gave his only Son, so that everyone who believes in him may not perish but may have eternal life. ' Indeed, God did not send the Son into the world to condemn the world, but in order that the world might be saved through him."

Jesus' disciples asked him to teach them to pray, to talk to God. In a wonderful model, Jesus made some things very clear. One of those is that we might expect to receive forgiveness of the sins we commit. He taught us to petition God in this manner: Forgive us our sins as we forgive those who sin against us. Of course, that adds a little something, doesn't it? The measure we receive will mirror the measure we give. God is magnificent in that way.

All that we have explored gives us cause to realize that Joel was on the right track. There is precedence throughout our salvation history to make Joel's remarks gospel and not simply wishful thinking. Personally such actions of God demonstrate for me how he is the same yesterday, today, and tomorrow. I see no God of the Old Testament and God of the New Testament. For us who struggle to get it right, to live and love as Christ loves us, to act instinctively rather than blindly adhering to the Law, Joel was absolutely right in his assessment. In those perilous times when we have sinned and recognizing our sin denounced it, "Who knows whether he will not turn and repent, and leave a blessing behind him, a cereal offering and a drink offering for the Lord, your God?"

Meditation on a Question found in Matthew 11:1-6

"Are you he who is to come, or shall we look for another?"

For us who are Christians in this day and age, this is an incomprehensible question. Even in the day it was posed, and by whom it was asked, it seems like a ridiculous question. John the Baptist had already confirmed the suspected identity of Jesus. Once he told his disciples that the man they were watching was the Lamb of God who takes away the sins of the world. John even questioned Jesus at the latter's baptism if he (john) wasn't the one who should have been baptized by Jesus.

Of course, John is in prison by now, and he, no doubt, was feeling depressed. That was not a term or concept of that day, but as we reflect on those times, John's incarceration, his being shut away from others in a dungeon like cell, he had to be in a state of depression. It was in that context that he wanted some reassurance that indeed Jesus was the one who was to come.

The world has a number of great, historical religions. Coming to mind right away are the Jewish and Islamic religions. Jews know the name Jesus, but I am not sure how they view him. I do know that he is not accepted by them as the one who is to come. They don't even ask the question that John the Baptist asked. The Muslims, I understand, consider Jesus to have been a prophet, and that is the extent of that. Other religions have their positions or lack thereof about the man Jesus.

Reading the scriptures, we can find the things that were supposed to be attendant to the Messiah or Christ. So much in the gospel narratives points to prophecies and to the fulfillment of them by Jesus of Nazareth.

Jesus taught with authority not like previous rabbis and teachers and preachers. He was certainly different. In his resurrected state, the men on the road to Emmaus remarked, "Didn't our hearts burn when he opened up the scriptures to us?" Speaks to the power in his word.

What things could help to convince one that this Jesus of Nazareth was the one who was to come? We have the necessary testimony. Jesus himself told the men to go and tell John that the blind see, the lame walk, the deaf hear, and the poor have good news preached to them. These are the things it is expected that the anointed of God would do. Jesus certainly filled the bill.

Clearly, as they say, the proof of the pudding is in the eating. What parallel to the eating of the pudding do we have about Jesus relative to his identity?

When the president of the United States of America travels in this country or participates in a parade—actually none has done this in a long time—but the presence of the Secret Service makes it abundantly clear that the president is in the area.

When the Pope participates in roadway pageantry, he can often be seen in his Pope mobile.

The very first sign that Jesus performed was turning the water into wine at a wedding. I gather that these were tricks that the magicians might not have been able to perform.

Jesus went to the little girl who had died, and he caused her to return to life. He even made sure the people saw her eating so that they recognized that this was a person and not a ghost.

Taking just the meager rations of a young lad, Jesus was able to feed thousands of men, women, and children. In today's world, it is hard enough for the average housewife to feed her family with expensive groceries she gets from the grocery store. Certainly what Jesus did is classified as a miracle.

What is interesting is that John tells us that Jesus did many more things than the ones he reports; however, it would take entirely too many pages to publish them all.

So, for many of us, it all comes down to faith. As we sing in that hymn, the Light of Christ has come into the world; the Light of Christ has come into the world. The creeds sum up what we believe about God, and a part of that confirms our belief in Jesus Christ as the Son of God, who came down from heaven, taking a body like ours, dying for us, and then being raised from death. We have no need to even consider another.

I love Jesus so much, and I understand who he is and what he does for us, and I just want to tell those who do not have this knowledge and understanding. I am totally convinced that he is the one who was to come, and I do not expect another. And even though some have religious belief, they do not have what we, followers of Christ Jesus possess: the fullest revelation of God in history.

In John's Gospel, he writes that no one has ever seen God; it is the Son who is close to the bosom of the Father who has made God known. No longer must we be in darkness about God. In Christ, we have seen the Father since he is in the Father and the Father is in him.

And deep down, John the Baptist knew that this man was indeed the one who was foretold. In fact, he had already attested to that fact previously. John was witness to the voice and the action of the Spirit when Jesus was baptized in the Jordan River. John had sent his disciples to follow Jesus. John had made a powerful confession. He said of himself, "I must decrease as he (meaning Jesus) increases. A clear indication that John not only understood his role, but he understood who Jesus is.

I'll answer that question for John. Yes, this Jesus is he who is to come." Further, you need not look for any other. How will you or how do you answer the question for yourself?

Meditation on a Question found in John 6:60-71

"Do you also wish to go away?"

This question came during a so-called teachable moment. Jesus speaking to a large group, apparently, began to teach on the merits of eating his body and drinking his blood. Let someone use that kind of language today in a group, and somebody would be looking at some serious lockup time in an institution. People would call the person speaking this way crazy.

Some of those listening to Jesus could not accept what he was saying. They considered the teaching to be hard or difficult. How do we see it in this day and age? And here I speak not only about these matters, but I speak about the subjects such as one finds in Luke 6. Jesus told us to turn the other cheek when we have been struck by someone. Jesus told us to love our enemies; and to do good to those who hate us. When someone takes our coat, we are to give them our shirt as well. Wait a minute! Can we handle these teachings? Forget the eating and drinking teachings because what we find in Luke 6 is almost impossible for a rational human being to handle.

In the area of forgiveness, Jesus gave us more wisdom. When he was asked about the number of times we should forgive our brother who sins against us, Jesus said that we are to forgive such persons seven times seventy-seven. In effect, we must forgive others indefinitely. Difficult teachings and admonitions? You betcha!

Who can accept such teachings indeed? That is the 64 thousand dollar question. Many of Jesus' disciples admitted that they found them impossible to accept. Where do we stand today?

As one who grew up in the segregated South, I recall an incident that occurred during my last regular high school football game. Here is the backdrop to this story. There were 22 high schools in Atlanta, Georgia when I was a senior. Six of those were for Black students exclusively; the other 16 were for the white students. Never mind that Black students made up approximately 51 per cent of the city high school population. Several of the white high schools had stadiums where they played their football games. The Black teams played in Herndon Stadium, which was owned by a local, traditionally-Black college.

My last game as a senior was to be played in Grady Stadium. It was the first time that Blacks had played in that stadium. We should have known that something was bound to happen. What happened was not really racial in fact. Our opponent was another Black team. But towards the end of the game, a fight broke out and resulted in both teams clearing their respective benches. I recall Marie saying to me that she looked out on the field and there I went trotting out there to "get hurt." According to our coaching staff and our principal, Mr. D. F. Davis, that was a shameful display. We had let the whole race down by our lack of discipline, our lack of self-restraint. The tension was so thick that one could have cut it with a knife. Mr. Davis said— and I'll never forget his words as he shook his fingers at us— "Fellas, what in the devil happened?" That was mild compared to what the head coach had in store for us once we returned to our school's gymnasium. His assistants never let him confront the team, however, which I confess to you averted a very ugly consequence. To further put this in context, I recall that the week before, a free-for-all broke out on a nationally-televised football game. It was as intense as our fight, at least. The combatants in that melee were none other than our future officers from the Army and the Naval academies.

All of that said simply makes the point that some things are just difficult to accept. Restraint is difficult to maintain in certain situations. Jesus gave us some hard sayings and he exhorted us to exhibit an unconditional love that is almost impossible to project. Indeed, who can accept such hard teachings? Who can hold back when the first punch has already landed on you or your friend?

Then Jesus turned to his small circle of disciples soon to be his friends. He asked them if they wanted to join the others, those who could not do what Jesus told them they should be able to do. Jesus asked them, "Do you also wish to go away?"

In the movie, *An Officer and a Gentleman*, Richard Gere's character, not being granted weekend liberty, has been forced to remain on base where Sgt. Foley gives him the business.

Continually badgering the Gere character, Zack Mayo, Foley asks for the DOR (drop on request) from Mayo. Finally Mayo sobs like a baby and said that he would not go away; he would not grant a DOR because he said, "I've got no place to go! I've got no place to go," he repeated. Not quite as dramatic, our man Peter answers Jesus' question. He says, "Lord, to whom can we go? You have the words of eternal life. We have come to believe and know that you are the Holy One of God." For Peter, like the Gere character, there was "no place to go."

Staying power. There will always be those who will have staying power. There will be those who can accept the hard and difficult teachings. There are those who can appreciate the benefits of adhering to the teachings of Jesus. Eating of the body of Christ and drinking his blood results in a wonderful benefit: abiding in Christ Jesus as he abides similarly in us. More important is the gift of eternal life for those so willing to partake of his Body and Blood.

Those early followers of Jesus really had to put their money where their mouths were, so to speak. That was particularly true in the early centuries of Christianity. Many were martyred. Many were betrayed by friends and family members. They were fed to the lions. They were forced to provide the entertainment for blood lusting Romans. But they persevered because they knew the identity of the man who taught those difficult teachings. They knew that having faith in Jesus and doing his will would bring about the ultimate prize for them. Jesus does indeed have the words of eternal life, and who doesn't desire that?

There were always self-appointed cheerleaders on the football teams on which I played. They were also self-styled philosophers. I will always remember those dreadful August days of practice in the heat, and I will remember that philosopher saying, "It's hard but it's fair." That's the way it is for those who follow Jesus. That's the way it is for those who adhere to the tenets of Luke 6. That's the way it is when one abides in Christ letting him abide in them. The rewards are great not only in heaven but in this life as well.

Do we also want to go away? I think not. Jesus has those important words of eternal life, and it doesn't get any better than that. No, we will not go away like some of those early disciples. Like Kizzie, we will stay put; we will run the race to its completion. We will fight the good fight. ¡Ultreya!

Meditation on a Question found in Psalm 130

"If you, Lord, were to note what is done amiss, O Lord, who could stand?"

There really could not be a more perfect passage of scripture for reflection than this question posed in one of the psalms we are reading each Noonday during Lent. It speaks to something that some of us miss. I am particularly focused these days on the self-righteous, and I hope that I am not among the ranks of those persons. Jesus spoke to his disciples and consequently to us about judging, or rather not judging. The point he wanted to make is that we will be judged by the same standards we use to judge others. Then he continues by asking, "Why do you see the speck in your neighbor's eye, but do not notice the log in your own eye?" *Matthew 7:3 Some* of our good friends are so wrapped around the axle about a particular occurrence in the church that they have forgotten their own sins. That is a clear and present danger I assert!

Since there is a truth here that suggests that we all will come under judgment, then we ought to be as gracious as possible towards our neighbor. We do not want to be like the policemen,

Inspector Javert, in the novel *Les Misérables* written by Victor Hugo. If you recall that book, the main character stole some bread to feed his child. He had no food at home and he had no money. The survival instinct took over automatically, and he acted inappropriately in one way, but courageously in another. Long story short, having been convicted and incarcerated, then being treated badly in prison, the man eventually escaped, and the remainder of the story surrounds this policeman's relentless pursuit of Jean Valjean. Inspector Javert, the policeman exhibited no grace towards Valjean even in the face of the convict's having spared his life. Because Inspector Javert could not overlook all that had happened to Jean Valjean, he drowned himself to avoid going against his duty. Judge not lest you be judged. That's what Jesus urged us to do.

I believe that those currently in our church who are almost violent in their opposition to the things that transpired at General Convention 2003 are on a path of destiny of being harshly judged themselves. The intensity of some reminds me of another question of the Bible: "Who made you a prince and a judge over us?" *Exodus 2:14*

What's at stake here? Simply put, the question posed by the psalmist is one more way to express what Isaiah proclaimed so eloquently. "All we like sheep have gone astray; we have turned every one to his own way; and the Lord has laid on him the iniquity of us all." *Isaiah 53:6*

Look at the two elements: (1) We are all sinners. Not a single person living can say otherwise. Can you? If I am in error, I'd like to hear from you. Look realistically at your own life. Sometimes anecdotal experience is compelling! (2) God has bestowed his grace on us. Remember that we say that Lent is about reflecting upon the grace that God has bestowed on us and the development of how we will respond to that grace. We have sinned; God has provided a remedy for our sinfulness.

Personally, for many years I have described myself during my childhood as being a good boy, one who did not get into any trouble. Most of that personal assessment is valid; however, the not getting into any trouble is not true. A few days ago, I was thinking about a deed that I had done in my childhood, and I heard myself exclaim, "That was awful!" I was not a good boy all the time. There were things in my life of which I am ashamed. In fact, my conscience is working to suppress the memory of the deed I just referenced to the point that I cannot even remember what it was that I did. Although we have been called to be perfect as the "Father in heaven is perfect," the fact remains that only Jesus lived as one of us yet without sin. No other person in history can make that claim!

The church fathers are wise indeed, and that's why tradition is so valued among some Christian Expressions (i.e., denominations). When we baptize people in the church, we take that opportunity to encourage all present to renew their baptismal vows. One of the renewal elements in that process is revealing. Here is a partial exchange between the celebrant and the people that illustrates the point:

Celebrant Will you persevere in resisting evil, and, whenever you fall into sin, repent and return to the Lord?
*People*I will, with God's help.

Notice that the question posed to the people does not say "if you fall into sin." It is a given that we will, and we will do so regardless of our maturity, or our relationship with Christ Jesus. So we say, "whenever you fall into sin." It is inevitable that we will miss the mark, which is another way of saying we will sin. So the question gets at the remedy for those times when we do sin.

As a new deacon in the church in 1990, I recall standing at the bedside of a woman in a nursing home, and pondering why I should say the Confession of Sin with her. Why, what evil could she have done? If one takes a look at the general confession we pray at major celebrations of the Eucharist, we will find the answer, in part. "We confess that we have sinned against you in thought, word, and deed, by what we have done, and by what we have left undone. We have not loved you with our whole heart; we have not loved our neighbors as ourselves." *The Book of Common Prayer* 360 That's a pretty broad framework in which sins can be and are committed by us—even those of us in some environments of restriction like a nursing home. And age and disability, we have seen most recently in the Chicago area, are not deterrents to our missing the mark at times.

The psalmist was so perceptive. He asked the real question. He has helped us to realize the truth about ourselves. In effect he has urged us not to think more highly of ourselves that we ought. One thing we could bear in mind is the parable of the Wheat and the Tares. That story makes it abundantly clear that God is firmly in charge of any judging that will need to be done. That said, we might spend more time looking at the log in our own eye, which clouds how we perceive the speck in our neighbor's eye. We might spend more time on our own knees talking to God about the things we have done and left undone.

We might spend more time affirming the truth of the psalmist: "If you, Lord, were to note what is done amiss, O Lord, who could stand?"

Meditation on a Question found in Mark 12:12-17

"Whose likeness and inscription is this?"

This question appears in the narrative in which some (notably the Pharisees and Herodians) were attempting to ensnare Jesus; to trip him up and cause him to misspeak. They prefaced their question with a number of truths that established the setting. In particular, they mentioned that Jesus was a truthful man, and that he was not concerned with anyone's opinion. This prefacing meant that they would force Jesus to say something that would put him in a bad light.

I know some people who are, pretty much by their own proclamation, a righteous people. They have the words of salvation. They seem to be the way, the truth, and the life. Perhaps that may be a bit judgmental on my part, but it is not far from the truth of how they feel about themselves. At least, that is how they come across to me.

A case in point makes the point, I believe. They do not under any circumstances drink alcoholic beverages. Given their strong objection to such drink in any fashion, you can just imagine what they think of the celebrations of the Holy Eucharist in which wine is used. One of that group spoke critically about the use of wine in cooking. He felt that was bad because alcohol could have a negative effect on those who ate food cooked with wine or beer for example. This man was not knowledgeable enough to understand that alcohol usually cooks out and dissipates during the cooking process.

I like jazz. I have since my early college days as an undergraduate when I weaned myself from so much rock and roll. Of course jazz is the true art form created in America. It has many expressions, and it can even be found in a useful and influential way in the liturgy. Such music, as are rhythm and blues, and others, are beneath these people.

They even have a slant on the correct version of the Bible. I don't remember which version they consider **the one**, but it is certainly not the *New Revised Standard Version*, which I use.

Those early Jewish officials held a repugnance towards their overseers, the Romans. They hated the tax collector who worked seemingly in a seamless fashion with the Romans to bleed the people. So, they asked Jesus if it was OK to pay taxes. That was a hot box kind of item. It's almost like asking if a man still beats his wife. How can one answer at all without incriminating himself?

But they did not know whom they were attempting to trip. Jesus practiced what he preached. Remember he told his disciples to be as wise as serpents but as gentle as doves. Jesus asked for a coin, and he asked them, "Whose likeness and inscription is this?" How crafty; how inventive! What a strategic question that was. Because the money has Caesar's image on the coin, it logically follows the money is his anyway. So Jesus told them, simply, to give to Caesar what belongs to him and give to God what belongs to God. How could he have gone wrong? He couldn't, and he didn't. They had to be amazed at the nimbleness and the verbal and mental agility of the man Jesus.

The lesson in this for us is that we are in the world and there are some things in which we will participate. Sure, we who are Christians are required to attend weekly celebrations of the Holy Eucharist, which is the principal service of worship for Christians on Sundays. Christians will be expected to support their local parishes in special observances; that might include weekday services and the like. Christians will be expected to be participants in some of the various ministries of the church. But note that Jesus is not requiring exclusivity. He does not require that we praise God unceasingly and at all times. He provides for us to be engaged in other activities, some even that may be worldly.

So, we will find Christians at the baseball field watching the Brewers, for example. We will find Christians in the local theaters watching *As Good as It Gets*, *Titanic*, *Barbershop*, as well as *The Passion of the Christ* or *The Ten Commandments*. Jesus told us that he came that we might have life and have it in all its abundance.

So, we cannot trip up modern day Christians because they engage in secular activities. In reality, almost everything thing is a spiritual matter because it is God who has given us the creativity, the skills, the gifts, and the resources to participate in some of the things other than so-called religious things.

There is an implied admonition, however. Notice that Jesus says we are to give to each according to whom it belongs. What belongs to Caesar, we return to Caesar; and what belongs to God, we give to God. The bottomline is that there seems to be a responsibility, an obligation even, to give.

April 15 requires that by that date all that live and move and have their working being in this country will have paid what is owed to Caesar or to Uncle Sam. The Catechism requires that each of us will "follow Christ; come together week by week for corporate worship; and work, pray, and give for the spread of the kingdom of God." *BCP 856*

I confess to you who hear or read these words that I have been true to what Jesus permits us to do. I still own my home. None has been taken away from me. That suggests that I have paid my taxes, and there are all types: income both state and national, property, sales, and the like. I have attended jazz concerts, and plays, and symphonies, and other concerts, and the like. In my life I have been observant of the rendering of things appropriately.

Finally, the story from which this question emanates tells us one other important thing for our life. Notice how the officials indicated that Jesus was not concerned with people's opinions. Of course, we all have opinions, and they are all over the place in import, truth, and validity. When we are doing what God would have us do, when our focus is on that image of God in Christ Jesus, we need not fear anything or any person. We simply must concentrate on giving our all to the relationship that exists between us and our God through Jesus Christ our Lord. Amen.

Meditation on a Question found in Exodus 14:10-18

"Is it because there are no graves in Egypt that you have taken us away to die in the wilderness? What have you done to us, in bringing us out of Egypt? Is not this what we said to you in Egypt, 'Let us alone and let us serve the Egyptians?'"

How myopic? I love that word because it describes unequivocally in so many cases the so-called human condition.

Here are the People of Israel who have slaved, literally, for years under the oppression of the Egyptians. Their enslavement was based on a false assumption, and they toiled for years in that tortuous condition. Joseph had been a marvelous savior of sorts to the Egyptian people, but when those who recognized his value died off, others decided that the greatly multiplied people of Israel were a threat to them. They conjured up many falsehoods about this people. And so they labored under the heavy hand of their captors.

Then as we know, God did a marvelous thing for the people. He coaxed his servant into service, and Moses followed the plan of God to set God's people free. Moses, under the tutelage of God, performed numerous and wondrous signs before Pharaoh the King. These were all done to show forth God's power and his determination to free his people. These acts were not done in the dark. The people were witnesses to these marvelous signs.

Especially they saw, later in our story, the mighty right hand of God at the Red Sea when God parted the waters to permit the Israelites to pass safely across that vast water. They saw too the power of the water as God released it from its walled state to engulf the pursuing Egyptian soldiers, chariots, chariot drivers, and horses. So utterly complete was Pharaoh's army decimated! And the people witnessed these great signs of God. How could they forget what they had seen?

That seems to be the story of humankind. We have a tendency to be myopic. In some situations that may be a good thing. That is if our shortsightedness causes us to forget painful experiences. Our physical hurts fall into that category. One summer when I was in college, I worked in a service station [For the young, that is a place where full service and care for automobiles are rendered]. While checking a customer's car, I opened the radiator cap, and scalding hot water made contact with my body—in particular my arms and my stomach. I was in pain for days before the pain finally subsided. At the time of my accident, the pain was so intense, I wanted to die. That's how great the pain was. But in time, the pain has become only a remembrance in my mind. Myopic in that case is good.

Who does not remember September 11? That was such a tragic day in the lives of every American. That cataclysmic event had the effect of bringing Americans, almost without exception, together in a state of unity never before seen or imagined. As I recently told some people in a conversation, I saw a preacher pray on a national newscast using the name not only of God, but Jesus the Christ. And because of the devastatingly horrible tragedy of that fateful day, I never heard a peep from those who would have normally been incensed by the utterance of prayer in that venue.

Alan Jackson, the popular Country and Western singer and superstar, gave some interesting insight into how we responded to September 11. In his song, "Where Were You When the World Stopped Turning," he asked if you went to church and held hands with some stranger, if you stood in line and gave your own blood? We were together; we were unified for a time. It was great. Paul spoke about there being no male or female; no slave or free, no Jew or Gentile, and the like. I say following that eventful day, there were no democrats or republicans, no Blacks or whites, no them and us among our countrymen. But those times appear to have abated, or rather the feelings we exhibited have gone away. We have gone more than two years past the event, and our memories are dulling.

I don't know if we rightly or wrongly criticize the efforts to combat terrorism, but I do know that we sound very much like the Egyptians once they had emerged from their state of captivity and enslavement. They even thought the old way was perfectly fine. Hear their questions again. "Is it because there are no graves in Egypt that you have taken us away to die in the wilderness? What have you done to us, in bringing us out of Egypt? Is not this what we said to you in Egypt, 'Let us alone and let us serve the Egyptians'" Isn't that how many of us now see the Patriot Act, the new procedures at the airports? Don't some of us question the wisdom of invading Iraq? Justified or not, we look very much like the myopic Egyptians of Moses' day.

The word in its optical sense is near-sightedness. I use it in a similar sense, i.e., short-sightedness. It could also refer to narrow-mindedness. In any event, that seems to be the kind of memory the Israelites were experiencing when they left Egypt. All the wonderful things God had done to effect their freedom, and they had forgotten them. You know that this people even went so far as to have Aaron fashion a God for them out of their jewelry. How short-sighted! Not too long before, their real God had brought them safely to freedom. But what do they do? They complain.

I have a tendency to be critical of some measures that have been implemented supposedly for the safety of us all. I know, for example, that I am not a terrorist. I do not even like to fly although I have flown countless times. So, it would be inconceivable that I would want to bring a plane down or do anything else in that sense. Some of the tactics simply bother me, and I complain.

People in Racine are seemingly very concerned with their school situation. But their myopia comes into play when they are not willing to pay for the education for their children. How long can one's taxes remain constant while prices for everything else around us continually rise? We seem to have forgotten that money is necessary to expose our children to various and necessary educational experiences. The real tragedy in this situation, however, appears to be that many of us have forgotten the real focus of public education: our children.

QUESTIONS FROM THE BIBLE

For us, there is a cure for this myopia. Our Lord Jesus Christ came down from heaven so that we might look farther into the future. He came that we might have new life. He came that we might have the ability to have a fresh start, and to have that again and again. I am hopeful that the message of Jesus can invade the hearts and minds of the many so that we need not complain like the Children of Israel. I am hopeful that we can abandon the myopic posture and look to Jesus who came that we might have life and have it in all its abundance. Myopia in a person can be compensated for physically through the use of optical lenses. Our optical lens for our souls, for our spirits, is none other that the one who lived, died, and rose for us. With Him there is a correction to 20-20, and we can see clearly once again.

Meditation on a Question found in Mark 10:17-22

"Good Teacher, what must I do to inherit eternal life?"

I am in just a bit of quandary about attaining the eternal life status. How does one really go about ensuring that he or she will have eternal life? Apparently I am not alone. There have been countless people in history who have sought the answer to longevity. The man in our Bible passage for this day was inquisitive in the same way.

For me, from my very early remembrances, I have felt I knew the secret to fulfilling my lifelong dream, i.e., to see God face to face. I am not certain as to when I knew this truth, but from an early age I have heard the beatitude that says, "Blessed are the pure in heart for they shall see God." That on the surface seems to be a simple and viable solution to the problem. That it seems to me is the formulary sought by so many throughout the ages.

We know that the beatitudes describe those who love the Lord with all their hearts, with all their soul, with all their minds, and with all their strength. We know these are they who love their neighbors as well as they love themselves. The beatitudes describe the holiness in those who are blessed of God. Their lives reflect these kinds of traits or characteristics. So in a sense, the beatitudes can be viewed as commandments for how we should live our lives. And for those, like me over the years, who wish to see God, it is imperative that we develop pure hearts. That means that we center our lives on God. That means that we walk in love as Christ loved us and gave himself for us, an offering and sacrifice to God. Blessed are the pure in heart for they shall see God. How easy in one way, how accessible!

It is amazing how we adopt certain things as youth, but I was extremely young when I knew that this beatitude was the way to see God, which means the bottomline is that I will have gained eternal life. Remember that Jesus said of little children that unless we come as a little child, we would not get into the kingdom. He also exhorted us to suffer the little children to come unto me and forbid them not for of such is the kingdom of heaven. For some, this just may be the way they should follow to gain eternal life.

The man approached Jesus and asked him point blank what he needed to do to gain eternal life. In the man's eyes, it was necessary that we must do something to gain such a prize. So, naturally, he went to the definitive source. Jesus rattled off a few of the commandments as being extremely important for one seeking admittance to the kingdom and thus to have eternal life. The man was seemingly proud to admit that he had been a long-time adherer to the commandments. In fact he goes on to boast that he had kept the commandments since his days as a youth. Surely that should have been sufficient.

However, Jesus gave the man one other thing to accomplish. Jesus told him that he lacked only one thing more. Wow! Suppose you were told that there was a single thing left for you to do, and you would ensure your presence in God's kingdom where you would stand in his nearer presence. What would you do? Could you live up to the challenge? The man speaking to Jesus could not go as far as Jesus suggested.

Jesus told the man to go, sell all his possessions, give the proceeds to the poor, then give up his regular life and become a follower of Jesus. The man being tied to his possessions—and they were many—left dejectedly. In the same way that Peter heard Jesus' words as the cock crowed on that faithful evening, I hear the words of Jesus as he said, "It is easier for a camel to go through the eye of a needle than for a rich man to get into heaven." Where do you stand in that regard?

I had a friend once who found upon the death of his wife that she had been a faithful giver to her church. My friend was upset that she had given not only to her church but also to other appeals for money. We have a tendency to become upset when our older family members begin giving away their money. The guise is often that they will give away their inheritance and the money they need on which to subsist. Could it really be that the inheritance just may not be as large as it could be if the person did not give it away, and that is the real concern?

This exercise helps me to understand that God has not provided just a single way to gain eternal life or salvation or entry into the kingdom of heaven. The entry points appear to be many in fact.

For example when Jesus told his disciples that he was going away to prepare rooms for all, one of the disciples, Thomas, did not know the way they would have to follow. Jesus told them, "I am the way, the truth, and the life. No one comes to the Father except through me." John 14:6

Jesus had a good friend, Lazarus, who died. The sisters of Lazarus were upset with Jesus because they felt he could have saved Lazarus. In response to Martha, Jesus told her, "I am the resurrection and the life. Those who believe in me, even though they die, will live, and everyone who lives and believes in me, will never die" John 11:25-26

The bottomline answer to the question the man asked of Jesus lies firmly entrenched in that passage of scripture we often refer to as John 3:16. "For God so loved the world that he gave his only son, so that everyone who believes in him may not perish but may have eternal life."

So why, then, was the answer given to the man about selling all that he had and giving the money to the poor and following Jesus? If we love someone, how is that love manifested? Do we simply want to harbor that love within our souls never to disclose it to the object of our affection? Do we simply want to have that good feeling and never express it in any way? Do we not want to make that love manifest for our object, and indeed in some cases, for the world to know of our great love?

In other words, for every action, there is an equal and opposite reaction. Cause and effect is one scientific way to put it. Love really is not love unless we give it away. Biblically,

James put it this way. Faith without works is dead. It naturally follows that being faithful followers of Jesus and setting our sights on the kingdom of heaven and eternal life means that we will be active in Jesus' earthly ministry. That means we focus less on our own pleasures and help bring the way, the truth, and the life to those in need. When we follow Jesus, that is our agenda.

So we must live out the commandments not simply observe them. If that means we sell all that we have, then so be it. In the final analysis, we will be taken care of now and in the age to come, we will be granted eternal life. Thanks be to God. Amen.

Meditation on a Question found in John 1:19-23

"Who are you?"

I couldn't help but have some fun with this meditation. Who are you? That's a loaded question. The first thing that came to my mind was a cartoon character from my past. He might have been at home here on Lake Michigan. He is the one who answered that question like this.

I'm Popeye the sailor man; toot, toot; I'm Popeye the sailorman; I'm strong to the finish 'cause I eats me spinach. I'm Popeye the sailorman. Toot, toot!

That same character was made to emulate God Almighty. Remember that God answered Moses, who had asked him his name, this way. "I am who I am." Exodus 3:14 And what did our loveable Popeye say? I yam what I yam and that's all that I yam. Just an echo of the almighty, wouldn't you agree?

"Who are you?" The question is quite a good one because it makes anyone who is asked that question attempt to define himself. It is always interesting that most of us think of ourselves in the context of doing rather than being. So when we are confronted with such a question, we give a response that says something about what we do. Typical answers include but are not limited to: I teach biology at the local high school; I sell cosmetics for Maria Kate; I write legal briefs for a law firm, and the like.

The question we are exploring was asked of John the Baptist. He was this strange wild man who had literally burst upon the scene, and he had the crowds in an uproar exhorting them to repent. He pretty much appeared to be a front man for someone else. He had a following, true, but he was more like an act that is used to warm up the audience for the main attraction. Because of his faithfulness and his tenacity, I suppose, the question about his identity naturally arose.

"This is the testimony given by John when the Jews sent priests and Levites from Jerusalem to ask him, 'Who are you?' He confessed and did not deny it, but confessed, 'I am not the Messiah.' And they asked him, 'What then? Are you Elijah?' He said, 'I am not.' 'Are you the prophet?' He answered, 'No.' Then they said to him, 'Who are you? Let us have an answer for those who sent us. What do you say about yourself?' He said, 'I am the voice of one crying out in the wilderness, "Make straight the way of the Lord,"' as the prophet Isaiah said." John 1:19-23

Another dimension was added by John. He told his inquisitors who he was not. Then he proceeded to tell them what he did. Of course that in part was because they ask him a parallel question: "What do you say about yourself?"

Is that really how we define ourselves? If so, who are you?

QUESTIONS FROM THE BIBLE

Those of us sitting in this room this afternoon say that we are Christians. If that is true, and if we accept the premise that we define ourselves through means of what we are doing, then there is a similar question posed to us. If being a Christian were suddenly made a crime—that's correct, against the law—then if you were indicted and brought to trial, could sufficient evidence be found to convict you of being a Christian, beyond a reasonable doubt?

Jesus approached this question from its other side. He knew that some wondered who he was. They had heard him teach and preach in the synagogue, in the fields, on the plain, in an intimacy with his closest disciples. Some even confessed that he spoke with authority unlike other authorities. They had witnessed the many miracles he had performed. Can you imagine what those present must have thought when they saw this man walking on water? They were present for many of the acts of healing he performed. Since they never asked Jesus who he was, Jesus posed the question himself. He said to his disciples, "Who do the people say that I am?" When he heard all the wild answers they presented, then he asked them, "Who do you say that I am?"

It is really difficult to say at any one time who we are. We are multifaceted people with various life experiences, so the answer changes constantly. I recall the story about a bunch of blind people who were told to hold onto an elephant. Because of the enormity of the animal, some were holding on to various parts of the elephant, for example, the ears, the trunk, the tail, the legs, and the like. Then they were asked to describe or tell what an elephant is based on their experience. It was difficult to realize they were describing the same animal. In that same way, humans are all over the place in the spectrum of identity.

If the question were asked of me, I might answer on one occasion that I am a child of God, or I am a man just attempting to get by. Makes me think of the little boy in *Children's Letters to God* who wrote, "I'm doing the best I can." If I were charismatic I might answer, "I am slain in the spirit." I am Marie's husband. I am a priest of the church. I am an American. I am a good citizen. If I were truly reflective and really mature in my outlook, I'd tell you that "I am a person being not doing." I write poetry. I am a photographer. I am a handsome, middle-aged, overweight man, and I lied about being middle-aged.

Who are you? What answer will you offer? Jesus said there will be those who will say "Lord, Lord." But he will not respond to them because he will not know who they are. Seemingly it is not sufficient to have just eaten at table with the Lord. Your identity must be a little broader than that. So, if you are knocking on the doors to the kingdom and you are asked, "Who are you?" how will you respond? Will your answer be sufficient for Jesus to recognize you? Will your heart be pure? Will you be a person who has lived a life of doing works as a result of your faith?

I know that my own life will probably not be enough to answer the question definitively so that I might gain entrance to the kingdom on my own. I seek God's grace as the missing element that will guarantee my entry. Remember Jesus was referred to as "the Lamb of God who takes away the sins of the world." I certainly will give him my sins to bear. By doing so, the weight of those sins will not hold me back and keep me from the kingdom. Then I could answer the identity question in any number of other ways. Who am I? Well, I am redeemed. I am saved. I am one who has been justified.

The bottomline for us all ought to be that when we are asked who we are, we will be able to give an answer that shows that we have been and are mindful of the summary of the law. That means our identity will demonstrate clearly that we love God with all our heart, with all our mind, and with all our soul. It will demonstrate clearly that we love our neighbor as we love ourselves, and that love will be the same that Jesus had toward us. We want who we are to be intricately enmeshed in our living out our faith in God. Who are you? Who am I? Let it be said or written that you are one in Christ and he is in you. Let it be said or written that you are ever mindful of others. Let it be said or written that you are a new creature and that you live and move and have your being in the Lord your God.

Finally, it is enough to recognize that when we answer the question, we can answer only in a way that speaks to the God that is in each of us. Notice we answer by beginning "I am…" A little bit of the divine has just become evident in your answer.

Meditation on a Question found in Daniel 3:13-28

"Is it true, O Shadrach, Meshach, and Abednego, that you do not serve my gods and you do not worship the golden statue that I have set up?"

This question of Nebuchadnezzar really falls into the category of a question we asked previously during this series. Remember we asked about ourselves, "If suddenly it were against the law to be a Christian, would sufficient evidence exist to convict you of that crime?" Nebuchadnezzar was asking the rhetorical question for he already knew the answer. He was sifting out the evidence. He was making sure that what he knew about the three young men was correct. He was giving them a chance to recant any allegiance to a god other than the one he had fashioned. Of course it was true that Shadrach, Meschach, and Abednego did not serve the king's gods nor did they intend to worship them!

That is faithfulness. In my youth, there was the elephant, Dumbo, and he was said to be 100 per cent faithful, I recall. That is true of these three about their worship of the one true God: 100 per cent faithful.

Before we could answer that question, we would need to take an inventory of gods that exist today. I think of those things that some might put ahead of the one True God.

For example, I knew a man once who was a high ranking military officer; in fact, he was the commanding officer of a major military base. When he retired from active duty, his true love became exposed. He loved this mistress more than he loved his wife. Of course, Christians put God above all earthly relationships, so that in and of itself is neither incomprehensive nor reprehensible. This man connected with his mistress daily when he could. He was blatant about her. As you might have suspected, this couple did not stay married after his obsession with this mistress. In retirement, he purchased a home near his obsession so that he could be with her daily, and last I heard, he was playing golf everyday of the week.

I must confess to you that once I put a God ahead of the one true God, ahead of my wife and my family. It was not difficult to fall into that trap. I call it a part of this phenomenon we are discussing because of the obsession. That appears to be the key. My mistress was not even a bad thing as playing golf is in and of itself not a bad thing. Once I hated computers, but in the late 70s, I discovered the power and the usefulness of these new instruments in their home or personal configuration, and I was struck with the bug.

I came home from work every day, and the time I spent with the family was the little time at dinner each day before I went to the room where I kept my home computer. I spent hours and hours teaching myself to program that machine. I practiced solving little problems to write software applications, I read magazines that included information about programming. I studied examples of common routines. I typed computer programs from magazines and books into my computer. I became a guru of sorts in the personal computer field, but at what cost?

What is it like to have the kind of faith exhibited by Shadrach, Meschach, and Abednego? What is it like to be faithful to God in the mode of that elephant—100 per cent? Who measures up?

I think about the story of Ruth. Remember she was faithful to her mother-in-law even after the men in their lives had all died. Naomi had strongly suggested that Ruth and her sister-in-law return home to their own people. The sister-in-law returned. Ruth refused to do so. Here's a snippet from the conversation Naomi had with her daughter-in-law, Ruth:

But Ruth said, "Do not press me to leave you or to turn back from following you! Where you go, I will go; where you lodge, I will lodge; your people shall be my people, and your God my God. Where you die, I will die—there will I be buried. May the LORD do thus and so to me, and more as well, if even death parts me from you!" When Naomi saw that she was determined to go with her, she said no more to her. Ruth 1:16-18

Jesus of Nazareth was faithful to God the Father. We even say it this way: He was obedient to the Father all the way to the cross even death on a cross. That is perseverance in faith. He had an opportunity to recant his faithfulness. He had a chance to "save his earthly life." But he chose otherwise.

There was a man who went off to war where he was injured and his arm was amputated as a result. When he returned home, a person speaking to the man said that this veteran had lost his arm. The veteran corrected that observation. He said that he had given his arm. Quite a difference, and that is what Jesus did in his faithfulness to the Father. He gave his life for us and for the many who followed him then and now.

During the early days and years of Christianity, before the Romans adopted the Christian religion, and during the time when they persecuted those who followed that slain man, we find numerous examples of faithfulness to Jesus the Lord. Although many, even bishops who were supposed to uphold the faith, fell to apostasy and recanted their allegiance to Christ Jesus, there are countless stories about men and women who went to their death rather than repudiate their relationship with the Lord. It is the kind of testing that we do not have to endure in these days, which I suggest is grace.

There was Arthur Ricks. He stands out in my remembrance from my childhood and my membership in the church of my youth and of my formation. Arthur Ricks seemingly was a simple man. I recall he was not one of The People. He did not work at the Post Office. He did not work for Atlanta Life. He did not own the Atlanta World newspaper. He was not a teacher or a preacher or a doctor. He rode the bus everywhere because he did not own a car. I wonder if he could drive. But this man did come to church every Sunday. He sang in the choir, and I am not sure how I remember this, but he paid his tithe every week. [My church published a list of contributors with the amounts they paid.] You could say he was religious in his faithfulness to

God and that characteristic showed forth in the life that he lived. Arthur Ricks was a good man, a faithful man.

I have some good news for you sitting here today. Many of you have endured these ramblings of mine this season as well as last. Only extenuating circumstances have kept you away and prevented your having heard them all. Easily you could be paying attention to mistresses in your life. I think about the plethora of such relationships: golfing, gardening, playing video games, sleeping, watching television, traveling, and the like. Notice that the mistresses of our lives are not bad things in and of themselves as we have stated. They are akin to money which is not bad; but it is the love of money that can be problematic.

The question the king asked the three young men is the same one we can ask of ourselves. Is it true that we do not serve and worship the gods that have been fashioned by humans? Is that true because we have been and are now ever faithful to the one true God who has been made known to us by God the Son who is close to the Father? You got it right, King. We worship God almighty, the Father of Abraham, Isaac, and Jacob; the God who brought his people out of bondage in Egypt into freedom; the Father of our Lord and Savior Jesus Christ. And him only do we serve. Let us say to the king Nebuchadnezzar—if I were in my childish state, "Put that in your pipe and smoke it—but as a mature believer, "Do with that truth what you will."

Meditation on a Question found in Matthew 3:1-17

"I need to be baptized by you, and do you come to me?"

In this story, John is giving the people the business about their need to repent and turn back to the Lord. In all probability, it is a usual day for him. What else did he have to do? He had no wife, no children, no household to maintain—He lived in the desert. He was not a wealthy member of society. He apparently was not well-educated, i.e., in the formal sense as in institutions of learning. He was itinerant. On the surface, he was not like the officials of the Jewish religion; especially he did not have their prominence and standing in the community.

But isn't that like our God to use the unlikeliest of people to do his work? Noah we know was a righteous man, but he did not stand out otherwise and in accordance with how people set standards. David was handsome, but he was small, a scrawny little fellow; it was this lad who was chosen to go up against the larger than life Goliath. Ruth, a Moabite woman, was chosen to be an example of faithfulness for us. Moses, who admittedly was weak in tongue, was the one God chose to confront the mighty Pharaoh and to assist in freeing the People of Israel from slavery in Egypt. Jonah, a self-styled procrastinator and self-righteous man, was selected by God to send the warning to the city of Nineveh. God chose a bunch of shepherds to herald the good news of the nativity of the Christ Child. Among the men that Jesus chose to be his very close associates and companions on the way, not a one can lay a claim on respectability. They were ill educated, if at all. They were common workers, particularly in the fishing field. One was even a dreaded tax collector. None of them would be our choice for such work in a religious enterprise. Saul was a Pharisee and he was an aggressive pursuer of those early Christians "to bring them to justice."

Remember, "You'd have no power over me had it not been granted from above," Jesus said. In that regard, certain individuals come to mind. He chose Abraham Lincoln to work for the continued unity of this nation, and to bring a sorry chapter in our national history to a conclusion. He chose Roosevelt to lead us in a tragic economic period in the history of this country. He chose Martin to lead a nation into her consciousness and to bring a second sorry chapter of our country's history to the beginning of a conclusion. And he is calling us to be engaged in the incomplete earthly ministry of Jesus, which is the reconciliation of the world to God.

What an unlikely set of people throughout history and down to this day we are and have been. John the Baptist was no fool; he understood who it was he was about to baptize, and he was grappling with the gravity of the situation. John knew his weaknesses, his shortcomings, and his sinfulness. How could it be that the one who proved to be spotless was going to be baptized at the hands of the likes of John? That, no doubt, was his question to himself.

One of the things we must keep in mind is how we are viewed by God. First, in the beginning when God created the heavens, the earth, all living creatures, including us, and all that is seen and unseen; he looked on his creation and pronounced it "very good." As flawed as we may be, God has a huge place in his heart for us.

Second, we speak of our salvation history. That is what we basically call the time of our existence since from the beginning of time and our creation. As we note in Eucharistic Prayer C, "You made us the rulers of creation. But we turned against you, and betrayed your trust; and we turned against one another." And still we were not utterly and completely destroyed by God. He has found ways throughout our existence to save us. When almost all people on earth were found to be corrupt, God found persons in Noah and his family to serve as the yeast for the continuation of the race. He even gave us the heavenly sign of his promise to not destroy us by water; he set his bow high in the skies.

From the beginning, he has given us prophets and sages to reveal his righteous law. I think of Moses the great Lawgiver. I think of the judges, and all those who labored to keep us on the path to God and a right relationship with him.

And in the fullness of time, he sent his only son, born of a woman, to fulfill his law, and to open to us the way of freedom and peace. I paraphrase the ultimate statement of God's love for us this way. "God so loved the world that he gave his only begotten Son so that all who believe in him might not perish but may have eternal life. For God did not send his son into the world to condemn the world, but rather that the world might be saved through him."

Of course, we ought not to think too highly of ourselves. Humility is still a good trait among us humans. But realism is important also, and we know that "Christ has no body on earth but ours, no hands but ours, no feet but ours. Ours are the eyes through which Christ's compassion looks out upon the world; ours are the feet with which Christ is in the world. Ours are the hands with which Christ blesses all people now. So, we go from our places of worship to be the Body of Christ in the world."

In the encounter between Jesus and John the Baptist, John questions why he is baptizing Jesus rather than having the event reversed as far as on whom the action is accomplished. Jesus says they need to do this in this way to fulfill all righteousness. It is a representation, however, of the role that we who follow Jesus will be or may be asked to play.

I am just a simple man. I am not able to speak well; I am not an eloquent speaker by any means. I do not have enough knowledge about the Bible. I am not that secure in my own faith. I am a sinner.

I have just begun a laundry list of excuses we might pose for not following through on some action that God wants us to pursue and implement. There are many others that spotlight our false humility. And still there are other statements about the rightness of doing something we think lies in the umbrella of another.

In the end of our story today, we note that John consents to the baptism of Jesus. That's an important moment. We are always capable of choosing; that's what it means to be made in the image of God. But do we like Mary of Bethany choose the better part? John did, and his reward was the witnessing of the voice of God who confirmed the identity of the person now baptized: "This is my son, the Beloved, with whom I am well pleased." What an encounter? That kind of experience awaits us when we are asked to perform some task for God in an unlikely situation, one that does not make sense on the surface. Let's hope that when so approached, we will be prone to "fulfill all righteousness."

Meditation on a Question found in Acts 2:1-13

"Are not all these who are speaking Galileans? And how is it that we hear, each of us in his own native language?"

There was a time when God seemingly spoke to his chosen people only. They heard the voice of God. They had numerous recorded encounters with the Lord and with his various angels. Through them and himself, he told men to do great things in our history.

He told Noah to build a ship large enough to hold the remnants of all living things and the basis for the continuation of that very life. In whatever language, God was understood by Noah.

He told Jonah to go to Nineveh and to speak a message of warning to the people of that great city, a city populous even by today's standards. We know how that episode turned out.

He spoke to the boy Samuel and urged him to listen to what he had to say to him.

He spoke to Moses and to Aaron, and sent them off on a mission of freedom.

He spoke at the baptism of his Son in the Jordan River. Some were able to discern what God said on that day.

God has spoken to the saints over the years of our existence, exhorting these extraordinary men and women to extraordinary moments in our history.

When God has wanted to communicate with his people, he has made it possible for the target of his action to hear him. There is no wonder then that on that Day of Pentecost, the birthday of the church, he made his words accessible to all in attendance. So whether one was Greek or Jew, a foreigner or native of one of the many outlying cities and towns, God made it possible for his good news to be received.

We can never forget the truth we speak in our prayer of consecration in Eucharistic Prayer C. We remember that in creation, God blessed us with memory, reason, and skill. That said, we have the ability to communicate with different peoples all around the globe. What a marvelous entity is the UN in that regard. There the nations of the world, most who have languages that are foreign to the many, sit at table to discuss issues affecting them all. And all hear in their own languages. The UN provides for translations of what's being said so that all can hear in their native tongue or some language with which they are familiar. Some of us may have bemoaned having to take Spanish, or French, or Latin, or German in high school; however, it is that kind of exposure that has created a love in some who have gone on to become translators in the world. In the close communities that are Europe, people tend to be multilingual. That close proximity has fostered the ability of many to speak and understand various languages as a matter of course. All of this experience helps us to talk to each other. We all hope that this ability will serve the world good in avoiding armed conflicts that have so decimated peoples and lands throughout our history. How is it that people of Latvia and Brazil and Spain and India and all the others can hear, each of them in their own native language?

We cannot say enough about the American Bible Society. This was the publisher of the *Good News* version of the New Testament of some decades ago. That was a revolution of sorts. American Bible Society translated the Bible for the basic understander and reader of the English language. I found myself turning to that version of the Scriptures for clarification of sticky passages in the Bible. That translation was most often clearer in rendering the meaning of the text. American Bible Society has composed translations in numerous languages, and now the Bible is available in so many lands around the world. People in the remotest outpost of existence can ponder how it is that they too can hear and read the same word that other inhabitants in the world can read and hear.

God has a plan for us his people. It may look like that plan has taken a long time to unfold, but a review of history shows the steady progression of God's revelation of himself to us. For example, once the Holy Spirit was selectively bestowed upon individuals that God chose to perform a given and specific task. Then on that Day of Pentecost, the Spirit became available to all, especially in baptisms, in which we are also rewarded with certain gifts of that same Spirit.

Jesus, in his earthly ministry, started out speaking in parables. His message was obvious to those who had ears to hear, but it was not so apparent to others. Jesus even said in a prayer that he was thankful that these things have been withheld from the wise. At a point near the conclusion of his ministry, Jesus told his disciples that he was now going to look on them as friends because he was telling them all that he had heard from the Father. He promised to speak plainly. No more interpretation would be required. No pondering of meanings would be required. What Jesus had to say would be plainly and directly stated. All ambiguity was removed as a result. Those friends may have asked how is that we hear the message clearly now?

In the fullness of time, it becomes time for revelation in various ways. In what is spoken is one of the ways that God has made his great love for us known. Things hidden now become visible to God's people. It is now the time that God wants to be known throughout the world.

The friends of Jerusalem were all together in a room on the day of Pentecost. It was at that time that God decided to bless his people with the Spirit. It came to those faithful followers with a sound that apparently aroused the inhabitants of the city. These were the witnesses to the speaking in various tongues that ensued. They should have known something exciting was imminent. Marie and I were on vacation in Washington, DC, during the last of the Nixon days in office. I have a wonderful 11X14 print of a large group of people just hanging outside the gate that surrounds the White House. There was an air of expectation, and people were just waiting. We expected something, and history reveals what happened to the president.

It is too bad that Oral Roberts was not living in that city on that day of Pentecost. It has always been his admonition to his listeners to expect a miracle. A miracle did occur on that day. The Spirit became accessible to all. God moved once more in the lives of his people. Another gift was given to and made available to all men and women and children. Just remember that it is the Spirit that is in the world today and in the church and leading us into all truth. There was confusion following the election at General Convention this past summer. But if we listen, we will hear once more the sound of the Spirit acting in the lives of the members of the church. And that Spirit will be leading us into all truth. That is a given, and in that we can place our trust.

We only have to listen to what God is speaking in our lives. We must do less shouting and more listening. God is speaking in a language that we all can understand. The day of Pentecost has had that rippling effect throughout our history. Because of that eventful day when the church was born, we need not vocalize that question anymore: And "how is it that we hear, each of us in his own native language?" for us it has become rhetorical.

Meditation on a Question found in Luke 24:13-27

"Was it not necessary that the Christ should suffer these things and enter into his glory?"

On the road to Emmaus, the risen Lord Jesus explained to a couple of pilgrims that what had transpired in Jerusalem were things that had been foretold. We always speak about birth pangs. In birth, there is an agitation and a commotion that necessarily accompanies the birthing process. What was born was new life in Christ for those who believe in him. What was born was life void of death. What was born was the way to salvation. All these things Jesus accomplished being faithful to the will of the Father all the way to the cross, and God raised him to new life. We who are baptized in a death like his will rise again in a life like his. That's the birth that was wrought, and it was accompanied by pangs. It follows that the answer is affirmative to the question raised in this meditation. Yes, it was "necessary that the Christ should suffer these things and enter into his glory."

A secondary question necessarily rises based on what we have said to this point. What is in store for those of us who follow Christ? There are some concrete answers to that question.

James and John, the sons of Zebedee, made a request of Jesus. You may recall that they wanted the privilege of sitting one on Jesus' right hand and the other on his left in his glory. Here is how Jesus responded to them:

"'You do not know what you are asking. Are you able to drink the cup that I drink, or be baptized with the baptism that I am baptized with?' They replied, 'We are able.' Then Jesus said to them, 'The cup that I drink you will drink; and with the baptism with which I am baptized, you will be baptized; but to sit at my right hand or at my left is not mine to grant, but it is for those for whom it has been prepared.'" Mark 10:39-40

Jesus tells those followers that they will undergo some form of trial. That would be the cup that he drinks as well as the baptism with which he is baptized. Martin Luther King, Jr. knew that truth especially when he was in Chicago. Another time, I heard him say to his followers "There are going to be some difficult days ahead." Some Christians have experienced the cup of which Jesus speaks. Some suggest they are experiencing that even as we speak, in this very day.

Given our most recent focus on the Passion of our Lord, I am reminded of what Jesus says in one of the Stations. In station eight of the traditional model of the way of the cross and in station nine in a version written by John Paul II, Jesus gives further suggestion of things lying ahead of us. He speaks boldly and definitively: "A great number of the people followed him, and among them were women who were beating their breasts and wailing for him. But Jesus turned to them and said, 'Daughters of Jerusalem, do not weep for me, but weep for yourselves and for your children. For the days are surely coming when they will say, "Blessed are the barren, and the wombs that never bore, and the breasts that never nursed." Then they will begin to say to the mountains, "Fall on us"; and to the hills, "Cover us." For if they do this when the wood is green, what will happen when it is dry?' "Luke 23:27-31

In another episode, Jesus goes even further in telling his disciples and us what will be required of those who want to follow him, who want to be his disciples.

Whoever loves father or mother more than me is not worthy of me; and whoever loves son or daughter more than me is not worthy of me; and whoever does not take up the cross and follow me is not worthy of me. Those who find their life will lose it, and those who lose their life for my sake will find it. Matthew 10:37-39

What else was foretold in scriptures about Jesus that underscores the fact that what happened was preordained?

Long ago the Prophet spoke in some detail about a suffering servant. We cannot improve on the words of his account, so I offer them to you unedited. Clearly Jesus fits this model.

See, my servant shall prosper; he shall be exalted and lifted up, and shall be very high. Just as there were many who were astonished at him—so marred was his appearance, beyond human semblance, and his form beyond that of mortals—so he shall startle many nations; kings shall shut their mouths because of him; for that which had not been told them they shall see, and that which they had not heard they shall contemplate.

Who has believed what we have heard? And to whom has the arm of the LORD been revealed? For he grew up before him like a young plant, and like a root out of dry ground; he had no form or majesty that we should look at him, nothing in his appearance that we should desire him. He was despised and rejected by others; a man of suffering and acquainted with infirmity; and as one from whom others hide their faces he was despised, and we held him of no account.

Surely he has borne our infirmities and carried our diseases; yet we accounted him stricken, struck down by God, and afflicted. But he was wounded for our transgressions, crushed for our iniquities; upon him was the punishment that made us whole, and by his bruises we are healed. All we like sheep have gone astray; we have all turned to our own way, and the LORD has laid on him the iniquity of us all. He was oppressed, and he was afflicted, yet he did not open his mouth; like a lamb that is led to the slaughter, and like a sheep that before its shearers is silent, so he did not open his mouth. By a perversion of justice he was taken away. Who could have imagined his future? For he was cut off from the land of the living, stricken for the transgression of my people. They made his grave with the wicked and his tomb with the rich, although he had done no violence, and there was no deceit in his mouth.

Yet it was the will of the LORD to crush him with pain. When you make his life an offering for sin, he shall see his offspring, and shall prolong his days; through him the will of the LORD shall prosper. Out of his anguish he shall see light; he shall find satisfaction through his knowledge. The righteous one, my servant, shall make many righteous, and he shall bear their iniquities. Therefore I will allot him a portion with the great, and he shall divide the spoil with the strong; because he poured out himself to death, and was numbered with the transgressors; yet he bore the sin of many, and made intercession for the transgressors. Isaiah 52:13—53:12

I would have thought that those persons who were contemporaries of Jesus would have been a little more in touch with the prophecy. What has become the Old Testament for us were the scriptures that were being preached and taught in the synagogues in that day. So events such as the crucifixion of Jesus should have been uppermost in their minds at that time. And it would not have been necessary for them to pose that strange question to Jesus (whom they did not recognize on the road.) They asked him, "Are you the only stranger in Jerusalem who does not know the things that have taken place there in these days?" Luke 24:18 But then, it was an emotional time for them. And then, too, Jesus' very close friends did not understand him when he told them all that would happen to him in Jerusalem. Grief, sadness, and sorrow have a way of dulling the senses and one's capacity to logic.

Suffice it that we can count our blessings if we are not being treated cruelly for that is not the case for some Christians around the world. At some point, however, it just might be necessary that we carry our cross in the same way our Lord carried his. The experience of Jesus, however, demonstrates clearly that we can endure anything in Christ; who knowing all that would befall him remained constant and faithful to the will of the Father; in Christ who fostered the creation of the great intersection between heaven and earth. Yes it was "necessary that the Christ should suffer these things and enter into his glory," and we are glad about that.

Epilogue

It is fitting as I began this series with the first question recorded in the Bible that somehow I should conclude with the very last question from this work. Obviously, the last question appears in *The Revelation to John,* which according to most configurations and versions of the Bible is the last book of the Bible. The question is "What city was like the great city?" Revelation 18:9-20, That verse refers to Babylon and her demise.

And so comes to a close, this exploration of some of the questions that are asked and answered by people who have had their lives chronicled for the entire world to experience. There really is no rhyme or reason to the questions per se. In other words, I paid no particular attention to their order. However, all these questions have a bearing on our salvation for the Bible is the record of our salvation history. It being a living document, however, the answers to the many questions can be answered again and again and by people in this day as well as those in bygone days. Who does not have a response to Pilate's penetratingly potent question, "What is truth?" The Philosophers have a field day with that kind of inquiry. Volumes and volumes literally can be written about that seemingly innocuous question. But it is in fact powerful as well as potent. What is truth? I am certain I did not do it justice in the space I allotted to it for my meditation in a thirty minute service that also included the reading of Psalms 120 thru 130 and prayers offered for a host of persons and concerns. What is truth? I hope people will ponder and provide the definitive answer. I'd love to hear it.

I suggested that questions were fashioned in many ways. Sometimes they appeared to be rhetorical. Reading these, you had to wonder why they were even asked. Some had answers that were apparent. Some questions were meant to throw the person being quizzed off track: Am I my brother's keeper?

One thing is certain. In the many questions asked, there is a representative of all the W's, i.e., Who? What? Where? When? and Why? The answers ranged from God to angels to Satan to Gentiles to Us and everything in between. What? Salvation, redemption, forgiveness, betrayal, love, war, lust, usw. Why? Why not? Because he loves us. When? In the fullness of time. On the night he was betrayed. Where? Everywhere. Ascended into heaven. Down to the pit. Questions, questions, questions, and their responses: answers, answers, answers.

A coherent theme? I think not. But then aren't questions just a way to keep the conversation going? The Bible tells us certain truths like "God so loved the world that he gave his only son." That statement elicits a multitude of questions: Who gave? What was given? Why was he given? Why did he wait so long? Was this a gift for the many or the select? What prompted God to act? What is meant by "world?" Does that include sinners? Why did the maker of heaven and earth have but one son? Why no daughter? What could his son do that he could not have done himself? And then given the few questions I could pose, think of all the people in the world and imagine the number of answers that are possible, from the obligatory "I dunno" to the elegant treatise and thesis.

This work is but a mere survey for there are far more questions than I could address in the 40-day period of Lent. Perhaps this can serve as a starter for someone who is willing to really present this exercise in its exhaustive format. Perhaps someone will be able to render the definitive answers to the Questions of the Bible. I look forward to the sequel or the true fleshing out of what I have begun in this work.

Who did what to whom, when, where, and why? Isn't that, after all, the question?

Richard Edwin Craig, III
The Day after Easter 2004

Appendix: Questions of the Bible

In this appendix are the questions answered in this book and some that were not actually addressed. This serves as a resource for those who may wish to answer some questions for themselves. Ostensibly Bible study groups might be interested in tackling such a project, but individuals should not shy away from this type enterprise.

Writing meditations about any subject matter from the Holy Scriptures is simply a way to appropriate what is found in the Bible to a person's life. If the Bible is a living document as many claim, then each person who attempts to answer the questions found in the Bible, for example, should be able to put a personal touch on the various subjects. That said, the possibilities for reflection are enormous. And the possibility for great variety is staggering!

Finally, only the surface has been scratched here. Obviously there are many more questions than are included below. So the definitive source for questions for exploration is found in the Bible itself. That resource is recommended to you.

The First Question Asked in the Bible

"Did God say, 'You shall not eat of any tree of the garden?'"
Genesis 2:4b-9, 15-17, 25—3:7

"Where are you?" Who told you that you were naked?"
Have you eaten of the tree of which I commanded you not to
eat?" Genesis 3:8-19

"I do not know; am I my brother's keeper?" Genesis 4:1-16

"Shall a child be born to a man who is a hundred years old? Shall
Sarah, who is ninety years old, bear a child?" Genesis 17:17-21

"Lord, wilt thou slay an innocent people?" Genesis 20:1-7

"Do you know Laban the son of Nahor?" Genesis 29:1-14
People are always trying to 'hook up' by showing some kind
of relationship

"What is this dream that you have dreamed? Shall I and your
mother and your brothers indeed come to bow ourselves to the
ground before you?" Genesis 37:1-11

"Who made you a prince and a judge over us?" Exodus 2:11-15a

"Who has made man's mouth? Who makes him dumb, or
deaf, or seeing, or blind? Is it not I, the Lord?" Exodus 4:1-12

"Is it because there are no graves in Egypt that you have
taken us away to die in the wilderness? What have you done to
us, in bringing us out of Egypt? Is not this what we said to you
in Egypt, 'Let us alone and let us serve the Egyptians'" Exodus
14:10-18

"What is man that thou art mindful of him, and the son of man that thou dost care for him?" Psalm 8

"My God, my God, why hast thou forsaken me?" Psalm 22:1-11

"I lift up my eyes to the hills; From where is my help to come?" Psalm 121

"Who knows whether he will not turn and repent, and leave a blessing behind him, a cereal offering and a drink offering for the Lord, your God?" Joel 2:12-16

"Is it true, O Shadrach, Meshach, and Abednego, that you do not serve my gods and you do not worship the golden statue that I have set up? Daniel 3:13-28

"Who is left among you that saw this house in its former glory? How do you see it now? Is it not in your sight as nothing?" Haggai 2:1-9

"I need to be baptized by you, and do you come to me?" Matthew 3:11-17

"Why are you afraid, O men of little faith?" Matthew 8:18-27

"For which is easier, to say, 'Your sins are forgiven,' or to say, 'Rise and walk?'" Matthew 9:1-8

"Are you he who is to come, or shall we look for another?" Matthew 11:1-6

"But who do you say that I am?" Mark 8:27-30

"Good Teacher, what must I do to inherit eternal life?" Mark 10:17-22

"What do you want me to do for you?" Mark 10:35-45
O the possibilities. Here is a man who can grant one's every wish, and he has asked, "What do you want me to do for you?"

[An open-ended question. No strings attached. The field is wide open. What does one request? See also Mark 10:46-52 for same question.

People often are not honest in these matters. Once I heard a bishop of the church say that if he won the Powerball, he'd spread the money among the churches so that priests could be placed without being concerned about monetary compensation.

How many times, when the jackpot of a particular lottery has grown extremely high, have you heard people speak about the altruistic things they would do if they won the big jackpot?

John and James and the blind man were all honest about what they wanted. That is not to say that those who purportedly would spend their winnings elsewhere are not telling the truth. It is all probably a matter of wining the lottery being an incomprehensible, unimaginable occurrence for the average person. If such persons actually won some big money, things just might be different.

Jesus said that he came that we might have life and have it abundantly. If he asks us what he can do for us, why would we not tell him what we really want?]

"Whose likeness and inscription is this?" Mark 12:12-17

"Is it I?" Mark 14:17-21

"For if they do this when the wood is green, what will happen when it is dry?" Luke 23:26-31

"Was it not necessary that the Christ should suffer these things and enter into his glory?" Luke 24:13-27

"Who are you?" John 1:19-23

"Can anything good come out of Nazareth?" John 1:43-51

"Do you want to be healed?" John 5:1b-9

"Do you also wish to go away?" John 6:60-71

Pilate said to him, "What is truth?" John 18:33-38

"Are not all these who are speaking Galileans? And how is it that we hear, each of us in his own native language?" Acts 2:1-13

If you, Lord, were to note what is done amiss,
O Lord, who could stand? Psalm 130:2

The Last Question Asked in the Bible
"What city was like the great city?" Revelation 18:9-20
Refers to Babylon and her demise

Lightning Source UK Ltd.
Milton Keynes UK
UKOW050122291211

184477UK00001B/196/P